STRIKE!

How the Furniture Workers Strike of 1911 Changed Grand Rapids

By
Jeffrey D. Kleiman

© Copyright 2006
Grand Rapids Historical Commission
All rights reserved

ISBN 0-9779043-0-X

Designed by Lynne Gort
Edited by Ellen Arlinsky

Printed and Bound by
Edwards Brothers, Inc.
Ann Arbor, Michigan

Table of Contents

Dedicated to all my family:
past, present and future

Preface

Former Speaker of the House Thomas P. "Tip" O'Neil once noted, "All politics is local," meaning that national political issues ultimately spring from the needs and concerns of individual constituents. In a similar way, all history is local. Our national past is the sum of local events played out by ordinary people every day. Historians may write about war or economic depressions in general terms, but horrors and hardships hit individuals and their families personally.

Without exploring the impact that larger developments have on smaller communities, and without presenting the ways in which individuals have perceived and dealt with change, historians cannot enrich our understanding of a particular time or place. The task of history is not merely to describe and analyze past events, but to provide us with the knowledge to face future decisions, to achieve a sense of place and purpose, and to understand the process of change over time.

This study of Grand Rapids in the Progressive Era is intended to offer ideas, provoke discussion, encourage further research, and create a context in which events took place. Often, we tend to think of the past as disembodied, unconnected to the present, with historical events left drifting in a sea devoid of reference points. We learn names and dates, read plaques, and study the inscriptions on monuments without appreciating their significance in the present, unaware of the links that connect them to our time.

When we look at Grand Rapids, or any local history, we explore in detail an important piece of the national fabric. There is enough diversity of experience across time and place that no single episode or group of actors can fairly represent the whole of the American experience; there is too much complexity and variation. Race, gender, occupation, religion, ethnicity, and countless other variables shape social interaction. Yet each local history contains a kernel of a larger truth, a reference point for comparison and contrast, which we can apply in other circumstances. In understanding that, we can seek to understand what has happened in Grand Rapids with a critical but sympathetic eye, and come to understand our place in the larger tapestry of history.

Acknowledgments

This history began as a doctoral dissertation at Michigan State University under the direction of Peter Levine and was helped along at the outset with funding from the MSU Urban Affairs program. The topic of urban reform was inspired by Zane Miller while I was a student at the University of Cincinnati and kept alive by the enthusiasm and votes of confidence repeatedly cast by Gordon Olson, now city historian emeritus of Grand Rapids.

Many other friends and colleagues helped see the project through to fruition. I was aided at every stage of research by the staff at the Grand Rapids History and Special Collections Center of the Grand Rapids Public Library, and when the research and writing were complete, Ellen Arlinsky edited the entire manuscript. Lynne Gort designed the book, Chris Gray produced the maps, and the skilled workers at Edwards Brothers, Inc. completed the work of publication. To all of them I am grateful for their careful, professional work. Finally, I wish to thank the members of the Grand Rapids Historical Commission for adding my account to the commission's series of books on Grand Rapids history.

The most important person in this entire process has been my wife, Kim E. Hartley, whose encouragement, support, and love have been compass points in my life. I offer the lessons about politics, religion, and economic change to my children, Asa and Dana.

I alone am responsible for the errors, limitations, and shortcomings that persist in this study despite everyone's best efforts to correct them.

Jeffrey Kleiman
Marshfield, WI
September 4, 2002

Introduction

From the end of the Civil War in 1865 until the beginning of World War I in 1914, Grand Rapids underwent a transformation shared by cities across the United States as the twin processes of urbanization and industrialism swept across the nation. So quick was this change that between the years of Theodore Roosevelt's birth in 1858 and his death in 1919, America emerged from its agricultural roots to become the greatest industrial power in the world.

Textiles made of wool and then cotton were among the first fruits of the industrial process. In the pre-industrial age, textiles were largely the product of individual workers, usually small land owners or tenant families, who depended on farming as their principal source of income and during the winter months used their own spinning wheels and looms to make fabric and then sell it to a merchant who would in turn resell it.

In the late 1700s, inventions in England such as the spinning jenny and the spinning mule altered the manufacturing process by allowing one worker to control multiple spindles or operate several looms at once to produce textiles in far greater volume than was previously possible. The ratio of output to worker jumped, and the cost of cloth declined. Gradually, with the introduction of machinery powered by various sources – wind, water, steam, and electricity – the factory system took root.

In the United States, the first small factories were established in rural towns, where land was relatively cheap, and often featured dormitory-style housing for the laborers. In many instances farm girls constituted a seasonal workforce, using their wages to supplement the family income, help pay property taxes, or perhaps put money away for a dowry.

Beginning in the early 1830s, large numbers of European immigrants, first the Irish, then the Germans and, later, groups from all over Europe, further altered America's nineteenth-century landscape. At its peak between 1870 and 1900, immigration was responsible for nearly one-third of America's population growth as wave after wave of newcomers streamed into the United States, many heading west, following newly built canals and railroads. Cities across the country became more populous, and demand for manufactured goods soared. Factories moved away from the countryside and into urban areas where labor became the least expensive and most easily controlled cost for any industrialist.

By the middle of the nineteenth century, as Americans increasingly bought factory-made goods, the older systems of compensation and exchange — barter, room and board, apprenticeship — gave way to cash, and money and wages assumed greater importance than ever before. Often lacking such marketable skills as knowledge of English and basic arithmetic, and not knowing how to operate industrial machinery, immigrants came to America with the belief that they could survive and care for their families by working hard and selling their labor for wages.

Although unskilled labor was the backbone of mass production, the large-scale industries that employed unskilled workers — meat-processors, steel plants, coal mines, refineries, and the like — often could not guarantee anything other than seasonal employment or work that fluctuated with the cycles of supply and demand in the marketplace. Because they could be easily replaced, wage-dependent workers often competed with one another for scarce jobs as good times turned to bad. Those with families were especially hard hit in slumping economies as children scrambled to find some sort of wage-paying work and wives augmented household resources by taking in boarders.

Of the many divisions that existed among the new groups of wage earners, the largest gulf was between skilled and unskilled. With fewer numbers, skilled workers, whether carpenters, joiners, plumbers, tool and die makers, hat makers, or other craftsmen, could more easily organize. They could control the supply of new workers by regulating the numbers admitted to apprenticeships, and they were higher up on the wage scale than their unskilled counterparts.

A second source of division was between immigrants and the native born. At the same time that millions of Europeans were arriving on American shores, many native-born Americans were leaving farms to seek their fortunes in cities. There they stood a greater chance than unskilled foreign workers of entering the skilled trades, advancing on the shop floor, or landing clerical and administrative positions.

Religious and ethnic differences further splintered wage earners. A profound anti-Catholicism characterized much of American society at the time. The growing numbers of Catholic immigrants from central and southern Europe encountered an anti-Catholic legacy of the English colonial period that found political expression in the Know-Nothing movement of the 1840s and continued through to the American Protective League in the 1890s. Suspected as a vanguard for papal conquest and the subversion of democracy, Catholics of any ethnic background were deemed suspicious at best and dangerous at worst.

Coupled with religious differences were the distrust of foreigners by Americans, the continued hostilities among immigrant groups carried over from Europe, and the insularity of immigrant neighborhoods and communities. Because the impulse to fragment remained stronger than the drive to find common ground, rapid assimilation and tolerance for diversity were not the order of the day. Ethnic gangs were common in cities of every size, and riots erupted occasionally in larger metropolitan areas, fueled by religious, racial, or ethnic tensions.

By century's end cities emerged as sprawling, energetic novelties resistant to traditional forms of local government and struggling under the weight of various burdens (marketplace regulations, inadequate public health and sanitation, poor air quality, rising crime rates) that had not existed to the same degree when the United States was dominated by a quilt of small-town, agrarian communities. The men who aspired to lead these new cities were not necessarily like earlier local leaders — scions of wealthy families whose social station had granted the privilege of education and training in law or theology. Rather, they were relative newcomers — industrialists and entrepreneurs who built their fortunes by taking advantage of opportunities in the rapidly expanding national marketplace and now wished to direct the continued development of their cities for the benefit of their fellow citizens as well as themselves.

To this new breed of power broker and politician, known collectively as Progressives, municipal governments often appeared to be out of control, allowing ballots to be purchased for a drink, a few dollars, or a political favor. The new leaders' distaste for these corrupt political practices ushered in the Progressive movement (1890-1917), which sought to produce political, social, and economic reforms compatible with the nation's new urban, industrial status. Attacking political party machines, child labor, sweatshops, and urban slums, progressive reformers promulgated such measures as the Sherman Antitrust Act (1890) and the Pure Food and Drug Act (1906) on the national level and supported laws regulating housing, labor. and welfare practices on the state and local levels.

At the heart of the municipal reforms was the notion that American cities should be governed in a modern, efficient, businesslike way. Progressive reformers proposed that professional managers under the direction of elected commissioners administer cities, rather than leave the job to political party functionaries. Popularly elected commissioners would set broad policy but not be involved in day-to-day decisions. Expertise and training would prevail to eliminate bartering favors for votes and put an end to widespread tolerance of urban vices such as gambling, drinking, and prostitution. Municipal workers would be selected on the basis of professional qualifications rather than friendship, political loyalty, or money donated for an election campaign.

The drive for political reform was aimed at the working classes. At its core was a set of moral values and a work ethic based on individual effort in which sobriety and good citizenship were rewarded with the privilege of voting and the right to limited participation in the decision-making process. Immigrants and dissatisfied workers who failed to mend their ways would find their political voice limited and their access to government reduced.

These tensions were nothing new. Similar debates and political battles existed from the mid-1830s onward as those in power sought to limit immigrant activities such as Sunday group socializing, frequenting saloons, and the preservation of native languages. The polyglot, culturally diverse tempest of city life frightened those who fervently believed that the United States could successfully exist only as a larger version of its Anglo-American colonial past.

The role of businessmen, bankers, and industrialists in reshaping city government to reduce the influence of ordinary voters was not surprising. These influential citizens had the resources — economic, organizational, legal — to turn their lesser numbers into an electoral majority. And they did not act alone. Their arguments appealed to large enough numbers of aspiring homeowners and others who shared the vision of an orderly and homogeneous society in which the poorer workers, many of whom were unassimilated immigrants, threatened hard-won gains. The immigrants' boisterous public behavior, devotion to native languages, different customs and religions upset those with longer tenure in America, generating support for a wide range of reforms that whittled away at the traditional structure of direct democracy.

The city of Grand Rapids, while not among the largest or oldest cities, mirrored the trends that characterized urban areas nationwide after the Civil War. The sudden expansion of its European-born population; the powerful link forged between its older economic fortunes and its current furniture-manufacturing industrial base; the collision of cultures in local politics; and a bitter labor strike all typify developments taking place across the nation during the years before and during the Progressive Era.

Chapter 1

Our Town:
Businessmen, Bankers, and the Pursuit of Control

On April 19, 1911, more than 3,000 furniture workers in plants throughout Grand Rapids walked away from their jobs in an effort to secure higher wages, shorter hours, better working conditions, and the right to bargain collectively. Joined by others in the following days, the strikers' numbers ultimately peaked at nearly 6,000. The roots of this largest and longest work stoppage in Grand Rapids history go back to the four decades that followed the end of the Civil War, in 1865, when the city's population, fueled by large numbers of European immigrants, grew from 15,000 to nearly 100,000, and furniture manufacturing became the city's premier industry. The impact of the strike was felt for decades thereafter, leading directly to dramatic changes in the city's economic and political structures. No other single event before or since has had such an effect on Grand Rapids.

Furniture City

Grand Rapids-made furniture first came to the nation's attention at the Philadelphia Centennial Exposition of 1876, a giant trade fair commemorating the 100th anniversary of American independence. Three Grand Rapids firms — Berkey & Gay, the Phoenix Company, and Nelson-Matter — brought elaborate displays that created a major sensation. The manufacturers were quick to promote their success, touting Grand Rapids as America's Furniture City and flexing their muscles at home, on their way to unprecedented influence and control.

From the 1880s to the 1920s, the furniture manufacturers dominated the political and economic life of Grand Rapids. They worked together to stifle competition from other local manufacturers, and they were able to distance themselves from regional and national banks through their adroit use of local banking institutions. They united in a series of mutually advantageous groups to control productivity, costs, and labor, and they attempted to squeeze out any troublemakers who, through unionization and other means, might introduce greater elements of unpredictability into the workplace.

The furniture industry outdistanced all other industries in the city despite the absence of any inherent advantages of location or resources. Grand Rapids stood removed from the major east-west rail arteries, and the long distances required to ship the finished product to market undercut any benefit conferred by proximity to Michigan's timber reserves. Waterpower from the Grand River played an important role in the city's early years, when the manufacturing base was more diverse. But in the late nineteenth century, the expanding furniture factories and other plants began moving away from the river, relocating along rail spurs and relying on coal-generated electricity or steam power.

The 1880s marked the beginning of America's transition from a rural to an urban nation. Over the next several decades, farming declined in importance and rural areas lost population to the nation's rapidly expanding cities, which by then were attracting great waves of immigrants from overseas. Urban growth created a tremendous demand for mass-produced, inexpensive household furnishings – bedroom suites, living and dining room sets and countless end tables, bookcases, and chairs.

At the same time, new office buildings punctuated urban skylines, providing a market for thousands of desks and filing cabinets annually. Sixty chain stores, including F. W. Woolworth of Philadelphia and S. S. Kresge of Detroit, operated nationally in 1900, and by 1910 the number jumped to more than 257.[1] The stores all needed display cases, and the case goods manufacturers of Grand Rapids gladly filled the bill.

The role of the furniture industry was essential to the economic health of Grand Rapids. In 1910, Grand Rapids was a city of 110,000 citizens. Furniture factories employed one-third of the city's wage earners, who turned out more than a third of the total value of the city's manufactured goods. Hundreds more local workers labored in furniture-related pursuits such as the manufacture of wooden and metal drawer pulls, hinges, and other essential fittings. Semi-annual trade shows staged by the furniture manufacturers lasted for six weeks at a time, dominating life in the city. Every January and every June, retailers, buyers, and salesmen of every sort poured into Grand Rapids from all across the country, placing orders, spending money, and boosting the local economy. The number of buyers attending these trade fairs jumped from 161 in 1893 to more than 1,500 in 1900 and continued to increase annually.[2]

By 1910 Grand Rapids, which ranked 44th in population among American cities, stood 42nd in a national list of 75 cities in terms of value added by manufacture. This ranking held enormous economic importance, gauging the degree to which skilled workers transformed raw products into something useful, and indicating the extent to which money was invested in the machinery necessary to aid in the transformation. Grand Rapids also commanded 39th place among the same 75 cities, and was 14th among industrial centers outside New

Comparative Growth of Four Major Industries in Grand Rapids, 1890 and 1910				
Type	No. of Firms (1890)	No. Employed	No. of Firms (1910)	No. Employed
Flour and Grain Mills	10	136	8	184
Foundry and Machine Shops	18	558	49	1,815
Furniture Manufacturing	31	4,347	54	7,854
Sawmill and Lumber Yards	12	629	20	709

(Source: State of Michigan Census Reports, 1890, 1894, 1900, 1904; Federal Census, Report on Manufacturers, 1910)

England, for the number of workers employed in manufacturing.[3] Thus ranked by the value of its products, Grand Rapids outshone larger cities such as Atlanta, Denver, Omaha, Portland, and Seattle. And when compared to other American cities on the basis of furniture manufacturing alone, Grand Rapids stood head to head with the five largest cities in the nation, turning out the tremendous variety of items needed to fill the houses, apartments, and offices of an expanding urban market. By 1880, furniture manufacture had become "by far the most important industry" in Grand Rapids, according to the Federal Census, and the city was "in fact the recognized center of the furniture industry in the United States."[4]

The Grand Rapids industry served all levels of the national furniture market. High styling combined with elegant hand-craftsmanship captured high-end customers, while efficient machine tooling and affordable prices supplied mass-market demands. Innovative uses for established products were another significant factor. John Widdicomb, for example, who broke away from the family furniture business he operated with his brothers to begin his own company in 1897, stepped outside the conventional market of office and home furnishings to solicit business from the Singer Manufacturing Company. Widdicomb secured a major order in 1901 for 200,000 five-drawer oak sewing cabinets, shipped at the rate of 2,000 a week at a profit of $8,000 or $4 apiece, the equivalent of $172,600 or $86.30 apiece today. Two years later he entered into a similar contract with the National Sewing Machine Company.[5]

Anchored by Campau Square, the intersection of Pearl Street and Monroe Avenue was the heart of downtown Grand Rapids and West Michigan's commercial center in 1910. These two postcard scenes from 1910 show the view from Campau Square looking north (above) on Canal Street (now Monroe) and south (below) on Monroe. (Grand Rapids Public Library, Grand Rapids Illustrated Collection, collection 91, box 3, folder 9. Hereafter cited as GRPL, with collection name, and box and folder numbers, eg. GRPL, 91-3-9.)

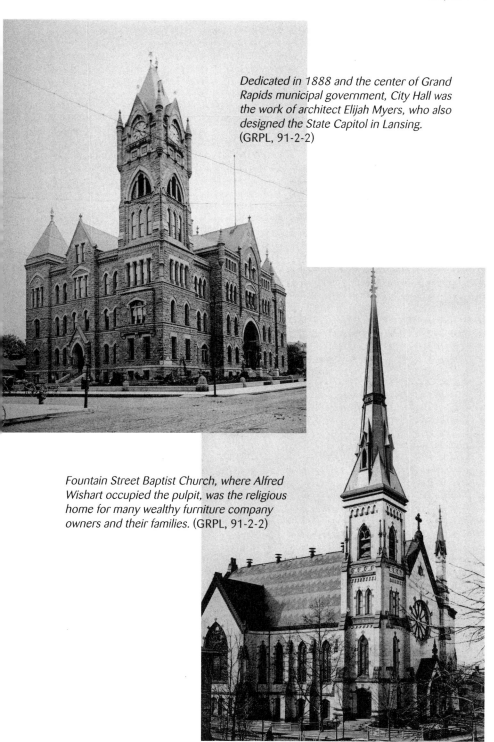

Dedicated in 1888 and the center of Grand Rapids municipal government, City Hall was the work of architect Elijah Myers, who also designed the State Capitol in Lansing. (GRPL, 91-2-2)

Fountain Street Baptist Church, where Alfred Wishart occupied the pulpit, was the religious home for many wealthy furniture company owners and their families. (GRPL, 91-2-2)

Only a short trolley ride from downtown, the hilltop district featured elegant late-nineteenth-century homes like these along Washington Street. (GRPL, 91-2-9)

Located in the heart of downtown at the corner of Fountain Street and Ottawa Avenue, the Peninsular Club had been the exclusive gathering place for Grand Rapids elite since it opened in 1884. (GRPL, 91-2-9)

Intersecting Interests

William Hovey Gay was born in Grand Rapids in 1863, the son of prosperous furniture manufacturer George W. Gay, and the grandson of pioneer settler and entrepreneur William Hovey. Despite his father's prominence, Gay started at the bottom of the furniture industry ladder, learning all aspects of the craft, from manufacture and sales to marketing and management, before becoming president of the Berkey & Gay Company, the city's largest furniture producer. Concurrent positions as president of the People's Savings Bank and member of the boards of directors of the Michigan Trust Company and the Fourth National Bank put him into proximity with the more powerful Kent State Bank and expanded his influence even further. He was the moving force behind the establishment of the local Furniture Manufacturers Association in 1881.

Gay's ties to the Fourth National and Kent State banks came through his business partner, John A. Covode, Jr., son of a Republican senator from Pennsylvania. The senior Covode gained national recognition in the years before the Civil War when he helped expose corruption in the Buchanan administration and discredit the Democratic Party. His son came to Grand Rapids as a 23-year-old college graduate and became a partner in a flour mill.

Both Covode and Gay were Baptists who attended Fountain Street Church and maintained memberships in the exclusive Peninsular Club. Their homes were barely a block apart in the Third Ward neighborhood now known as Heritage Hill. Covode's connections at Kent State Bank brought him and Gay into contact with Alexander Hompe, who had been born in upstate New York, attended Cornell University, moved to Grand Rapids in 1891 at the age of 26, and worked his way up the ladder to become vice president of the Royal Furniture Company. In 1900, he joined forces with Robert Irwin, president of the Phoenix Furniture Company, to purchase a controlling interest in the Royal firm. Irwin was one of the most prominent of the local furniture men, serving as chairman of the city water commission in 1907, heading the Grand Rapids charter commission in 1912, and later becoming president of the local Furniture Manufacturers Association.[32]

Like many of their other fellow industrialists, Hompe and Irwin lived in the hilltop residential area overlooking downtown and the factory districts. From their lavish homes, they could look across the river to the working-class neighborhoods on the West Side, and they were in short walking distance of the Peninsular Club. Connected to one another through business and banking interests and an informal network of social and business clubs, they wielded enormous influence throughout the city.

Rationalizing the Marketplace

Aggressive leadership by Widdicomb and his fellow furniture men changed furniture manufacturing in Grand Rapids from merely *one* industry into *the* industry. But furniture — along with automobiles, appliances, and other high-ticket items — falls into a category called consumer durable goods. The local market could consume only a limited number of bedroom sets or tables, and if the city's furniture manufacturers wanted to assure continued growth in the long term, they could not expect to rely solely on markets in and around western Michigan.

Continued profits required expansion beyond local and regional outlets to the wider horizons of national and international markets. But in competing for national and international customers, Grand Rapids furniture makers faced other manufacturers whose resources outran their own. Industrialists in other, larger cities had access to better transportation, more banks with more money to lend, and a larger pool of employees who could be pressed to work for lower wages in response to intense competition for jobs. As a result, Grand Rapids firms had to manage their affairs adroitly or be drowned by more strategically placed competitors in cities with more diverse economies and greater capital reserves. In short, aggressive Grand Rapids businessmen had to find some way to place what they did, and where they did it, on a par with businessmen in larger cities working from positions of greater advantage. The Grand Rapids furniture men set out to create a level playing field in national markets by insuring a greater degree of special advantage at home.

This quest for advantage was not unusual in an economy as volatile as that of late nineteenth- and early twentieth-century America. Businessmen across the country were involved in a process of consolidation. Pressed by the need to increase stability in the marketplace, regulate competition, and control production in order to survive, the leaders of large corporate enterprises often formed associations in pursuit of these goals.[6]

At the same time, bankers tried to control monetary supplies and capital markets that fell prey to the same unpredictable conditions facing industrial producers. For bankers, money is something to buy and sell for the greatest profit possible. Bankers "buy" money by offering to hold it for a lower rate of interest than they lend it out or "sell" it, and the tighter the controls on the money supply, the harder it is for smaller banks to compete.

During the late nineteenth century, manufacturers and financiers alike sought to curb seasonal irregularities in the availability of ready money. They preferred a system in which the demand for money and the rates charged for its use were less erratic. When bank assets were tied up in loans and mortgages endangered the entire drive for industrial expansion.[7] If individual bank depositors, prompted by panic or recession, suddenly sparked a run on the bank by insisting on withdrawing their money immediately, there would be no money available for business loans. Bankers had to be sure that there was money to lend and that there would be money enough coming in to keep on lending. Until the creation of the Federal Reserve in 1914, no system had been devised for tracking the amount and availability of money at either the regional or national level.

By controlling the money supply and imposing order and predictability on the process of manufacturing, transportation, and sales, bankers and industrialists sought to secure an effective rationalization of the entire marketplace. Seeing political power as a necessary ingredient in their quest for their version of a rational, predictable marketplace, they created trade organizations to protect their interests. But while sales and manufacturing associations could exert pressure, they could not compel compliance. Only government could do that. So it became vital to businessmen and bankers that they write regulations that government would eventually enforce.

Nolo Contendere

Taking a page from their peers across the nation, the financiers and industrial leaders of Grand Rapids undertook deliberate and determined efforts to dominate the local economy by controlling the ups and downs of the furniture industry. The intense competition of a national market, coupled with erratic swings in the economy, drove local manufacturers to search for stability. United by a common need to control costs and establish steady, predictable income levels, furniture manufacturers in the decades after 1880 moved to centralize information about their employees, suppliers, shippers, and markets, as well as to consolidate their purchasing power. In this way they could negotiate freight rates with the railroads and take steps to regulate wages and working conditions.

Nineteen firms formed the heart of the Grand Rapids furniture industry, accounting for one quarter of the city's entire labor force and more than 85 percent of its furniture workers. Larger than other local manufacturers, and generally more stable, these powerhouses had upwards of 6,000 employees. Less vulnerable to seasonal cycles in employment, wages, and production, these employees, unlike those in smaller shops and mills, could look forward to steady employment eleven or twelve months of the year.[8]

The nineteen leading firms, with the exception of American Seating, were locally owned and privately operated by two dozen or so men, with few outside influences in the form of public investment or absentee ownership. Taken as a whole, the number of privately held companies in the Grand Rapids furniture industry was three times greater than the average for the state of Michigan. On the opposite side of the ownership coin, the number of companies seeking public investment was less than half the statewide average. Retaining such a high degree of control over their factories was essential to the Grand Rapids furniture producers' success.

By the turn of the century, all of the city's major furniture-making firms were active in the Grand Rapids Furniture Manufacturers Association (FMA), founded in 1881. One of the nation's earliest trade associations, the FMA bargained with railroads over freight rates, handled insurance claims, and dealt with dishonest or insolvent dealers. Its two trade publications, the *Furniture Manufacturer and Artisan* and the *Michigan Tradesman,* served as official organs for furniture producers everywhere. Reaching a wide audience through national circulation, the *Artisan* and the *Tradesman* featured articles about production and worker safety, touted "scientific management," and kept firms across the country in touch with each other, recording information such as promotions, business successes and failures, and the deaths of prominent leaders.[9] Editorials regularly pleaded the case for stability in the marketplace and rationalized production.

From the beginning, the Furniture Manufacturers Association was a tightly knit group of local business owners exercising influence over their city and their industry. By the turn of the century, the FMA was a significant player on the national stage, using its influence to control prices and limit production. In the early 1920s, the Grand Rapids furniture men held such tight control over their industry that they were the targets of a federal investigation for possible violations of the Sherman and Clayton anti-trust acts.

The government's principal charge of price fixing addressed a successful attempt by the industry's larger companies to kill competition nationwide by arranging for all furniture producers to charge a minimum price for their goods. In the face of this price "floor" agreement, no one entering the field of furniture manufacture could undercut the big factories. Such clearly illegal actions within the furniture industry had been flagged by the government as early as 1898; the federal suit in the 1920s merely drew attention to operating procedures that had grown unchecked for a generation. More than 10 percent of the firms named in the federal government's suit against national manufacturers were located in Grand Rapids. Pleading *nolo contendere* (no contest, an effective admission of guilt), the manufacturers paid the fine rather than incur mounting legal costs or the additional scrutiny that would result from continuing to fight the charges.[10]

The Grand Rapids furniture manufacturers also created their own, privately funded Employers Association in 1905 in competition with the publicly run State of Michigan Free Employment Bureau established that same year. Like its government counterpart, the Employers Association functioned as an employment agency, placing workers when and where they were needed according to the shifting seasonal demands among the various furniture factories. Operating their own agency enabled the furniture men to meet their industry's specialized need for skilled workers without having to go through the larger, more generalized labor pool available through the state agency.

The organization did much more than allocate skilled labor among the city's furniture factories in a timely and efficient manner. According to the association's official charter, its stated goals included inhibiting unionization and using all means to preserve the "sacred and private relationship" between employer and laborer rather than relying on any arbitration imposed by outsiders.

The Employers Association kept a file on every worker who had ever been employed in the city's furniture factories in order to monitor wages, productivity, and union sympathies among workingmen. Among its self-appointed tasks, the Employers Association determined which employees were "competent or worthy" of employment; provided encouragement to its members "in their efforts to resist the compulsory methods sometimes employed by organized labor" to unionize a shop; and used the threat of a blacklist to keep workers in line. The association also promised to "protect its members... against [state] Legislative, Municipal and other political encroachments" on their professional autonomy.[11] In other words, the association sought to prevent government from authorizing workers to organize and bargain collectively. The connection between the manufacturers' private employment agency and their resistance to government intrusion could not be more apparent.

The Grand Rapids furniture manufacturers' close-knit fraternity also worked to police its own members by assuring uniformity of wage levels and discouraging competition among companies for skilled workers. One example of this control concerned a disgruntled worker who left one company to seek a job with another. He had received $2 per day on his former job and asked the new company for $2.25 per day without mentioning his old wage rate. The following day he was informed that $2 was all he had gotten and all he could expect to get.[12] Presumably any complaint he might have raised would have blacklisted him as no longer "competent or worthy" to continue working in Grand Rapids.

In a further attempt to bend the local economy to their own advantage, the furniture manufacturers worked hard to stifle efforts to organize their laborers. Initially the prospect of unionization involved only skilled laborers, but limited as that may have been, it still posed a double threat to the manufacturers. First, it would have provided a counterweight to the control owners exerted in the workplace, forcing them to abandon unilateral decision-making about wages and hours and making it necessary to share power with their employees. Second, union membership would draw in national support for collective bargaining. Despite the conservative nature of craft unionism, which restricted its membership to a few highly skilled wage earners, collective bargaining represented a dangerous first step to challenging the furniture manufacturers' authority.

Natural Allies

Owners deemed access to and control of money critical to keeping their large manufacturing plants flexible enough to respond to changing market situations. Just as they used the threat of blacklisting dissident employees to battle labor organizers and dealt with national rivals through powerful trade associations, the furniture factory owners sought to reduce their dependence on large regional banks in Chicago, Detroit, and New York by creating hometown alternatives. One effective strategy was to accept seats on the boards of directors of the principal commercial banks then operating in Grand Rapids. For example,

William Gay served as president of the board of the People's Savings Bank while also acting as a director for the Fourth National Bank and the Michigan Trust Company. At the same time, five of the city's largest furniture manufacturing companies were interlocked, through the directorships of their owners, with the Kent State and Grand Rapids Savings banks, which were also interlocked with each other. The Kent State Bank, in addition, stood directly interlocked with the Old National and City National banks, whose combined assets approached $2 million.[13]

Furniture company owners also created a second tier of financial institutions, assuring themselves of a ready supply of money for loans and credit needed for seasonal expansion. The years between 1905 and 1911 saw the chartering of three new local banks – City Trust and Savings in 1905, Kent State Bank, which had ties to the Michigan Trust Company, in 1908, and Grand Rapids National City Bank in 1911 – with furniture executives at their command. The manufacturers sitting on the boards of directors and in the executive offices of these new banks represented major local furniture concerns, each employing more than two hundred workers. Through their banking connections, they were able to play a major role in shaping monetary policy to their own advantage. [14]

A similarly cozy arrangement also saw the furniture men serving on each other's boards of directors. The Oriel and Berkey & Gay companies, which accounted for over 800 employees between them, shared executives William Gay and John A. Covode, Jr. The Phoenix and Royal companies were part of a tightly knit consortium headed by Robert Irwin and Alexander Hompe. Between them, these two sets of interlocking directorates employed about 1,200 workers, almost 20 percent of the city's furniture workers and nearly half of the workers in the employ of the city's nineteen largest firms. Because Grand Rapids firms were the nation's largest, it was estimated that at one time these four interlocking firms held at least 15 percent of the national furniture market share.[15]

Among the city's nineteen leading furniture companies, eight firms formed a special inner circle of power, with their leaders seated at the heart of a series of interlocking furniture and banking directorates.[16] These eight interconnected companies, with the exception of Berkey & Gay, which had holdings in excess of a half million dollars, had tangible assets in 1910 ranging from about $100,000 to $300,000, the equivalent of $2 million to $6 million today.[17] The eight firms were neither so big in terms of tangible assets nor number of employees that they could survive on a national level or dominate the local one unless they cooperated to control the marketplace. Their clout was best exercised collectively.

The eleven excluded firms, a more diverse group, were larger on the average than the other eight, with tangible assets ranging from $300,000 to more than a million dollars. Although these eleven companies were "independent" from the other eight, they were nevertheless bound to the industrial, financial, and mer-

Breakdown of Major Firms Interlocked and Excluded			
Interlocked Companies	**No. Employed**	**Independent Companies**	**No. Employed**
Berkey & Gay	454	American Seating	631
Phoenix	434	Grand Rapids Show Case	569
Widdicomb	405	Sligh	424
Grand Rapids Chair	387	Michigan Chair	394
Oriel	385	Luce	360
Macey	360	Michigan Cabinet	285
Imperial	285	John Widdicomb	269
Royal	207	Gunn	252
Total	**2,917**	Stickley Bros.	251
		Nelson-Matter	214
		Valley City	211
		Total	**3,860**

(Source: *Grand Rapids City Directory, 1912; State of Michigan Bureau of Labor Reports,1910, 1911, 1912; State of Michigan Banking Commission, Reports, 1910, 1911, 1912.*

cantile community by membership in the FMA and the influence they could wield in the number of wage earners employed.

A pervasive network of interlocking directorates allowed the eight-firm inner circle to share information about prices, policies, inventories, and cash availability, and to benefit immeasurably from their insider information. It also allowed the Grand Rapids banks to exercise a virtual monopoly in their region. When the Clayton Anti-Trust Act of 1914 outlawed interlocking directorates, banks and their directors had the option of applying for an exemption. More than five percent of the total number of directors denied exemption across the entire United States came from Grand Rapids, an astonishing figure out of all proportion to the city's size and economy.[18]

It is difficult to say with absolute assurance how the furniture men exercised their influence in the banking community. On the one hand, long-term and short-term investment in loans and mortgages by the "new" banks after 1905 did not differ significantly from the pattern set by older Grand Rapids banks. Nor did the proportion of money committed to loans, as opposed to mortgages, bonds, and securities, see any significant change. But the total amount lent for short-term purposes, especially by the "new" banks of 1905-11, suggested that money went to deal with the cyclical demands of the marketplace and seasonal demands in expenditures for raw materials, shipping, and storage. In absolute terms, the "new" banks accounted for nearly half of all capital reserves committed to short-term loans.[19] In any event, control of the new lending institutions assured the manufacturers of favorable loan rates and terms of repayment and guaranteed that the money they needed would not be drained off to "outside" interests.

Bankers controlled the flow of money in their cities through the formation of clearing houses. The most famous was the New York Clearing House, but all across the country clearing houses coordinated the difficult business of tracking cash and settling balances on a daily basis.[20] In Grand Rapids local banks created a clearing house not merely to facilitate the transfer of business drafts and other instruments, but also to lend a hand to local industrialists.

Established in 1885, the Grand Rapids Clearing House by 1900 had become a permanent fixture on the city's financial scene. Its chief officers and board of directors were drawn from three of the four commercial banks in Grand Rapids and, later on, from one of the three "new" banks. Although no furniture men served in any executive capacity at the clearing house, the interlocking influences continued to prevail. For one thing, as the member banks cooperated in keeping track of the balances owed to each other and to "outside" banks as well, the Grand Rapids Clearing House could coordinate the flow of loans so that no member bank would ever come up short when pressed for immediate payments. The cash settlements and management of money flow at the clearing house helped to keep adequate cash reserves in the vaults of the city's banks to meet the needs at hand.[21]

Manufacturers often pledged their factories as collateral to insure repayment of their loans, and their capital investments – machinery, raw materials, building expansions – effectively became fixed assets of the bank.[22] This gave the bank an interest, if not an actual voice, in the company's operation, turning the lender into a *de facto* investor, a silent partner making sure the company was successful enough to repay the loan. What neither party wanted, of course, was an irrational marketplace. In times of panic, one bank could call in loans it had made to other banks, forcing demands for the immediate repayment of business loans. Calls for the money to be repaid all at once would curtail manufacturing, throw men out of work, interrupt production, and begin a cycle of economic recall that would lead to recession – or worse, depression.

Across the nation, the years after 1905 were especially unsteady, with panics and recessions occurring in 1908, 1910-11, and again in 1913-14. Bankers and businessmen were natural allies during these troubled times, each with an important stake in restoring an environment where the demands upon money were predictable and orderly. For Grand Rapids furniture manufacturers, it made sense to insure friendship and share control of the city's available financial resources. Without successful management of the money supply, the recall of loans in times of "financial stringency" would result in pressure to liquidate bank assets and swiftly "disarrange the entire industrial system."[23] Ample inducement existed for cooperation among furniture manufacturers and bankers alike to rationalize their respective marketplaces.

Home Sweet Home

As immigrants poured into the country, residential construction grew dramatically in the United States in the years after 1880. Streetcar suburbs spread outward from older city centers, and small houses went up on tiny lots. Home ownership signaled an important step on the road to success, and family energies were harnessed to purchase and maintain this hallmark of achievement and respectability. In the years between 1890 and 1910, an increase in housing construction nearly doubled the nation's outstanding mortgage debt for private homes. On a per-household basis, this increase translated into a family debt ranging from $289 to $316, quite a burden when families relied upon contributions from every member to bring in an average income of $700 a year. The ratio of mortgage debt to income, as measured by the federal government and reported in the census, remained steady between 1890 and 1910 and showed the degree to which families were willing to borrow against some large measure of future income in order to own a home.[24]

On the eve of World War I, nearly half the homes in Grand Rapids were owner-occupied. A great many of the homeowners were Dutch and Polish, the very same groups that made up the largest percentage of the furniture workers. The majority of their modest homes were mortgaged to local banks and savings and loan organizations. This brought the wage earners into contact with Grand Rapids' industrial and financial communities after payday, creating an economic symbiosis that connected the two ethnic groups to one another and tied them even more closely to their employers.[25]

As the demands for housing increased after the turn of the century, privately owned banks could not keep up with the demand for workers' mortgages and other long-term debts. Throughout the United States, a pattern of wage-earner dependence upon sources such as workers' savings associations emerged. In Grand Rapids, the city's two largest savings and loans, the Mutual Home and the Grand Rapids Mutual Savings associations, had 5,000 active members, a figure

Growth of Housing Stock in Grand Rapids

	1-Family	2-Family	Multiple-Family	Total
1890 - 1899	3,577	2,738	429	8,879
1900 -1909	4,617	2,757	539	9,678
1909 -1919	4,843	1,628	410	7,893

National Increase in Non-Farm Housing

1890 - 1899	294,000
1900 - 1909	361,000
1909 - 1919	359,000

(Sources: Federal Census, Report on Housing, 1940)

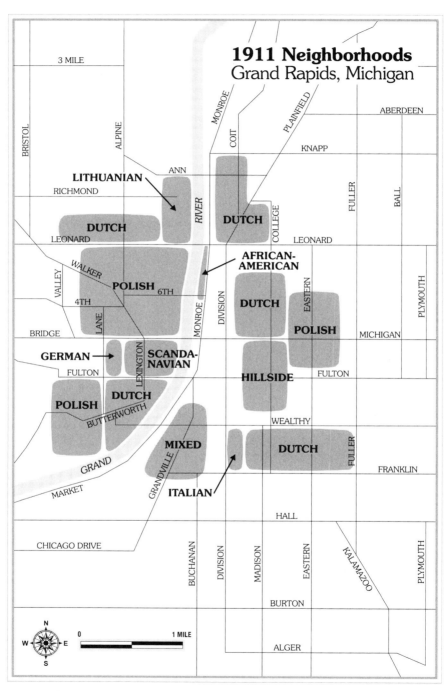

Home to thousands of European immigrants, Grand Rapids had several ethnically distinct neighborhoods at the beginning of the twentieth century.

representing 90 percent of *all* the city's residents enrolled in such institutions. Much of the remaining 10 percent belonged to the West Side Savings and Loan and the Valley City Savings and Loan, likewise vital sources for mortgage money to homeowners.[26] Unlike the major commercial banks and lending institutions, these organizations were smaller, neighborhood operations ostensibly run by and for the working class. Nevertheless, they, too, were tied to the established network of money and capital markets and could not avoid being subject to the same pressures affecting the city's businessmen and manufacturers in their pursuit of money for investment, expansion, and profit.

As the number of homes increased in Grand Rapids, the influence of the banks and the furniture manufacturers rose accordingly. Grand Rapids' chief savings and loans shared officers with the major banks and furniture factories, as in the case, for example, of the Mutual Home and Loans Company. Mutual's president, John Mowat, enmeshed the mortgage company in the financial interests of the National City Bank, where he served as a director, and the Grand Rapids Chair Company, where he was vice president. Any pretense that the city's five separate savings and loans associations competed with one another or stood apart from the major banks ended in 1911 when it was announced that the mortgage companies would pool their resources into a single fund.[27]

Control of the city's savings and loans gave the furniture men ready access to additional capital reserves created by workers' savings and made wage earners and homeowners even more dependent upon their employers. One-third of the city's wage earners trusted the security of their employment to a single industry, while even more workers fed their savings into the pool of capital dominated by industrialists seeking funds for expansion or other commercial investment. As money for mortgages and other long-term loans became tied more closely to other capital markets on a regional and national basis, workers had to rely on the banks to use their money wisely. But the banks in Grand Rapids were linked directly to the furniture manufacturers, who were doing their best to keep most of their own financial dependency limited to the local money market. If push came to shove and both businessmen and workers wanted to draw upon the city's available capital reserves for their respective needs, it would clearly lie within the industrialists' interests to expand commercial loans at the expense of worker mortgages and loans.

Dependence was even greater for those wage earners who had already committed themselves to long-term debt in the form of home mortgages. Attempts to challenge the manufacturers for better working conditions could result in blacklisting and the threat of no job, no home, and the burden of debt. The worker might even be denied access to his savings if the banks had lent the money to commercial borrowers. By 1911, the Grand Rapids furniture workers had become involuntary partners in financing the companies they worked for, but they were consistently denied any voice in determining wages, hours, or working conditions.

The Outsiders

Creating a powerful network enabled local industrialists and financiers to build a base of social and economic power while avoiding the larger national influences that dragged down many other small or regional producers. Grand Rapids furniture manufacturers also had the strength to hold at bay any outside influences that threatened their dominance in their own city. For example, during the years of urban industrial expansion in the early twentieth century, two outside firms tried to settle in the city with differing degrees of success. The American Seating Company of Illinois and the Brunswick-Balke Company of Ohio arrived as the drive for consolidation by influential local businessmen was peaking. Both newcomers were interested in the same labor pool and to some extent the same markets that served the local furniture manufacturers, who did everything in their power to curtail the abilities of the two companies to operate in Grand Rapids.

The American Seating Company arrived in 1902 through its purchase of the Grand Rapids School Furniture Company, an older, established plant. Although the newly formed company's principal headquarters remained in Chicago, the sale did not excite comment in the newspapers or professional journals, perhaps because the new owners were quick to continue membership in the Furniture Manufacturers Association and did not recognize unionized workers.[28] Nevertheless, American Seating remained an outsider, never fully accepted by the local inner circle because it was a member of the "seating trust" – so-called by the Grand Rapids manufacturers in a derogatory way – that included several companies around the country.

Even more strained relationships characterized the dealings between Grand Rapids manufacturers and the Brunswick-Balke Company, which came to Grand Rapids in 1904. Incorporated in 1901 as a merger of three Ohio firms, the company originally sold billiard and pool tables, along with bowling alleys, pins, and balls. Four years after coming to Grand Rapids, its product line had extended into the field of refrigerators and case goods. Because Brunswick competed for the services of carpenters, joiners, and other skilled woodworkers, the established manufacturers eyed the interloper with suspicion. Furthermore, shortly before deciding to come to Grand Rapids, Brunswick-Balke had recognized the right of workers to organize and bargain collectively. It had become a closed shop, employing only unionized workers represented by the United Brotherhood of Carpenters and Joiners, the largest and most influential union in the American Federation of Labor.[29] On two counts, then, Brunswick-Balke represented a threat to the city's self-styled business leadership.

In 1905, the firm employed 143 workers, a number that jumped threefold by 1907, and in 1911 Brunswick-Balke paid wages to more than 700 men. Had such a large closed shop become firmly rooted in Grand Rapids, local manufacturers would have faced a more difficult time in maintaining control of their own labor markets. Thus, when Muskegon promoters paid Brunswick-Balke a cash bonus of $72,500 to relocate to their city in 1910-11, local officials made no effort to match the offer. Grand Rapids Board of Trade leaders announced they had never felt "the need to give bonuses to get the right kind of people to come here," and never would. "The plants we want are the plants that do not need, or ask for alms."[30] Read another way, the closed circle of Grand Rapids industrialists and bankers did not welcome any corporation that failed to endorse their version of a special hometown interest in controlling labor, costs, and production.

Neither locally owned nor controlled, and with access to outside capital, American Seating and Brunswick-Balke were suspect in the eyes of the city's industrial leaders. Loyal to corporate headquarters in other states and dependent on money markets in Chicago and New York, these potential rivals might offer higher wages, thus upsetting local control over the labor market. Such fears were not unfounded. A special report of the Grand Rapids Board of Trade in 1916 found that hundreds of skilled workers were leaving Grand Rapids for better-paying jobs in automobile plants in Detroit, Flint, Pontiac, and elsewhere.[31]

The powers that guided Grand Rapids' economic life often made decisions over a drink at the Peninsular Club or a round of golf at Kent Country Club, and their close-knit arrangement required strength in numbers. Acting in concert, the furniture men had established the Furniture Manufacturers Association to oversee production and prices, maintained their own employers association to monitor wages and union sympathies, assumed control over local banks to tap the capital reserves of the city, and saw to it that their mutual interests intersected in a series of interlocking directorates. The furniture manufacturers' belief that what was good for them was good for Grand Rapids rationalized the concentration of economic power into the hands of an influential few.

Endnotes

1. Sidney Ratner, Richard Sylla and James Soltow, *The Evolution of the American Economy* (New York: Basic Books, 1979), pp. 376-79.
2. Twelfth Federal Census, *Manufacturers,* p. 84. For a history of the Grand Rapids furniture industry see: Richard D. Kurzhals, "Initial Advantage and Technological Change in Industrial Location: The Furniture Industry in Grand Rapids, Michigan" (unpublished Ph.D. dissertation, Michigan State University, 1973), p. 117; Allan R. Pred, *The Spatial Dynamics of U.S. Urban-Industrial Growth, 1800-1914* (Cambridge: MIT Press, 1966); Frank E. Ransom, *The City Built on Wood: A History of the Furniture Industry in Grand Rapids, Michigan 1850-1950* (Ann Arbor: Edwards Brothers, Michigan, 1955); and James Bradshaw, "Grand Rapids Furniture Beginnings," *Michigan History* 52 (Winter, 1968), 279-98; "Grand Rapids, 1870-1880: The Furniture City," *Michigan History* 55 (Winter, 1971), 321-42.
3. Twelfth Federal Census, *Manufacturers,* p. 84.
4. U.S. Bureau of the Census, *Special Bulletin,* no. 18; Department of Commerce and Labor, *Census of Manufacturers,* pp. 11, 13.
5. Ransom, *City Built on Wood,* pp. 51, 53. For comparisons of current and historical dollar values, see John J. McCusker, "Comparing the Purchasing Power of Money in the United States (or Colonies) from 1665 to Any Other Year Including the Present," *Economic History Services,* 2004 <http://www.eh.net/hmit/ppowerusd/>.
6. The literature is extensive, but best summarized by Edward C. Kirkland, *Dream and Thought in the Business Community* (Ithaca: Cornell University Press, 1956); Samuel P. Hays, *The Response to Industrialism* (Chicago: University of Chicago Press, 1957); Gabriel Kolko, *The Triumph of Conservatism* (New York: Quadrangle Books, 1962); Robert Wiebe, *The Search for Order* (New York: Hill and Wang, 1967); Alfred D. Chandler, *The Visible Hand* (Cambridge: Harvard University Press, 1977).
7. Kolko, *Triumph of Conservatism,* pp. 146 ff.; Robert Wiebe, *Businessmen and Reform* (Cambridge: Harvard University Press, 1962), pp. 154 ff. For a closer look at the process of management and self-regulation, see Jonathan Lurie, "Private Association, Internal Regulation and Progressivism: The Chicago Board of Trade, 1880-1923, as a Case Study," *American Journal of Legal History* 16 (1977), 215-38.
8. Employment information taken from Michigan State Census Reports, 1890, 1894, 1900, 1904.
9. Complete runs of the *Furniture Manufacturer and Artisan* and *Michigan Tradesman* are available at the Grand Rapids History and Special Collections Center of the Grand Rapids Public Library.
10. William Letwin, *Law and Economic Policy in America: The Evolution of the Sherman Anti-Trust Act* (New York: Random House, 1965); Federal Trade Commission, *Report on the House-Furnishings Industry* (Washington, D.C., 1923), v. 1, pp. 51, 54, 143, 407.
11. *Grand Rapids News,* April 19, 1911, p. 12; *The Observer,* July 7, 1911, p. 1.
12. Viva Flaherty, *History of the Grand Rapids Furniture Strike* (n.p., 1911), p. 21.
13. *Report of the Commissioner of the Banking Department of the State of Michigan* (Lansing, 1912).
14. Z.Z. Lydens, *The Story of Grand Rapids* (Grand Rapids: Kregel Publishing Co., 1966), pp. 304-305; *Report of the Commissioner of Banking,* 1912.
15. Federal Trade Commission
16. Linda Ewen, *Corporate Power and Urban Crisis in Detroit* (Princeton, N.J.: Princeton University Press, 1978); Mark S. Mizruchi, *The American Corporate Network 1904-1974* (Beverly Hills: Sage Publications, 1982); Michael Allen, "The Structure of Interorganizational Elite Cooperation: Interlocking Directorates," *American Sociological Review* 39 (1974), 394-407; Peter C. Dooley, "The Interlocking Directorate," *American Economic Review* 59 (1969), 314-23; Wiebe, *Businessmen,* pp. 95-97.
17. *Thomas' Register of American Manufacturers* (New York: Thomas Publishing Co., 1914), pp. 2374-79.
18. *Michigan Investor,* v. 15 (September 30, 1916), p. 12.

19. *Report of the Commissioner of Banking,* (Lansing, 1912); Lydens, *Story of Grand Rapids.* State reports give the aggregate figures only.

20. James Cannon, *Clearing Houses: Their History, Methods and Administration* (New York: D Appleton and Co., 1900), p. 14.

21. The emergence of local and regional markets in competition with national markets has been discussed by John A. James, *Money and Capital Markets in Postbellum America* (Princeton: Princeton University Press, 1978); Richard Sylla, *The American Capital Market 1846-1914* (North Stratford, New Hampshire: Ayer Publishing Co., 1979).

22. James, *Money and Capital Markets;* Herman E. Kroos and Martin R. Blyn, *The History of Financial Intermediaries* (New York: Random House, 1971); Paul B. Trescott, *Financing American Enterprise* (New York: Harper and Row, 1963). State banking reports do not provide detailed seasonal demands for capital, only the aggregate figures. The annual figures, while aggregated, do provide for some analysis on the nature of long- or short-terms loans.

23. Cannon, *Clearing Houses,* p. 14.

24. Leo Grebler, *et al., Capital Formation in Residential Real Estate* (Princeton: Princeton University Press, 1956), p. 164; Olivier Zunz, *The Changing Face of Inequality* (Chicago: University of Chicago Press, 1982); Matthew Edel, Elliot D. Sclar and Daniel Luria, *Shaky Palaces* (New York: Columbia University Press, 1984); *Report of the Immigration Commission* (Washington, D.C., 1911), v. 15, pp. 487 ff.; Paul Douglas, *Real Wages in the United States 1890-1926* (Boston: Houghton Mifflin Company, 1930); Albert Rees, *Real Wages in Manufacturing 1890-1914* (Princeton: Princeton University Press, 1961).

25. *Report of the Immigration Commission* (1911), p. 531; Department of Commerce, Bureau of Census, *Mortgages on Homes: Report on the Results of the Inquiry as to the Mortgage Debt on Homes Other Than Farm Homes at the Fourteenth Census* (Washington, D.C., 1923).

26. Figures are based upon *Reports* of State Banking Commissioner for 1910. The specific membership rolls are as follows: Grand Rapids Mutual Home Building and Loan, 2,577; Mutual Home and Loan, 2,957; West City Savings and Loan, 466; Valley City, 352; Grand Rapids Savings and Loan, 163.

27. Mizruchi, *The American Corporate Network;* Ann R. Marusen, "Class and Urban Social Expenditure: A Marxist Theory of Metropolitan Government" in William K. Tabb and Larry Sawers, eds., *Marxism and the Metropolis: New Perspectives in Urban Political Economy* (New York: Oxford University Press, 1978), pp. 90-112; Grand Rapids *Evening Press,* October 28, 1911, p. 15.

28. *Moody's Manual of Industrial and Miscellaneous Securities,* (New York: John Moody & Company, 1908).

29. *Moody's Manual,* 1904, 1908, 1911; Robert Christie, *Empire in Wood* (Ithaca: Cornell University Press, 1956); Morris A. Horowitz, *The Structure and Government of the Carpenters' Union* (New York: John Wiley and Sons, 1962).

30. Michigan Department of Labor, *Annual Reports,* 1900, 1902, 1904, 1908, 1911; Minutes of the Grand Rapids Board of Trade Board of Directors Meetings, June 1911, January 1912. Bound copies in the Grand Rapids Public Library.

31. Minutes of the Grand Rapids Board of Trade Board of Directors Meetings, June 13, 1916, p. 7.

32. Grand Rapids *Herald,* June 28, 1953.

Furniture City

From the late 1880s to the early decades of the twentieth century, furniture factories dominated the Grand Rapids industrial landscape. This gallery features images of some of the best-known companies.

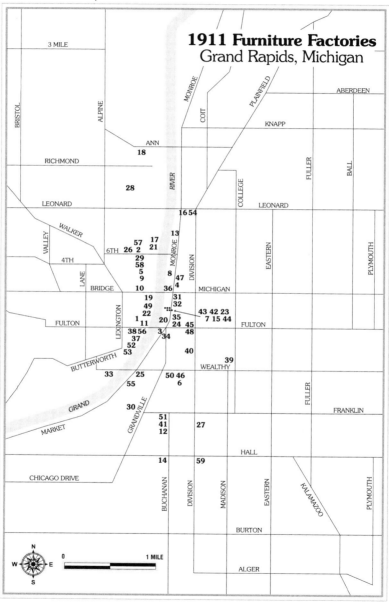

Grand Rapids was home to more than 50 furniture companies large and small in 1911. Most were located along both sides of the Grand River, with a few spread alongside railroad lines entering the city from the south. The numbers on this map correspond to the list of companies on the following page.

Furniture Companies, Grand Rapids, Michigan 1911

1. Adjustable Table Co., 45 Mt Vernon NW
2. American Seating Co., 901 Broadway NW
3. Wm A. Berkey Furn. Co., 39-55 Market NW
4. Berkey & Gay Furn. Co., 442-448 Monroe NW
5. Buiten, Doezema & Co, 12 Dewey NW
6. Century Furn. Co., 34-46 Logan SW
7. Colonial Furn. Co., $212^1/_2$ Pearl NW
8. Criswell Furn. Co., 519-523 Monroe NW
9. Fritz Mfg Co., 15-35 Alabama NW
10. Grand Rapids Art Furn. Co., 238 Front NW
11. Grand Rapids Bungalow Furn. Co., 8 Scribner NW
12. Grand Rapids Cabinet Furn. Co., 900 Grandville SW
13. Grand Rapids Chair Co., 901 Monroe NW
14. Grand Rapids Fancy Furn. Co., 1201 Steele SW
15. Grand Rapids Furn. Co., 109 Monroe NW
16. Grand Rapids Showcase Co., 100 Coldbrook NW
17. C.A. Greenman Co., 42 Seventh NW
18. Gunn Furn. Co., 1820 Broadway NW
19. Haney School Furn. Co., 250 Front NW
20. Heyman Co., 47-61 Monroe NW
21. Imperial Furn. Co., 750 Broadway NW
22. Johnson Furn. Co., Front and Pearl
23. Keil-Anway Co., 18 Huron NW
24. Charles P. Limbert Co., 47 Ottawa NW
25. Luce Furn. Co., 655-675 Godfrey SW
26. Luxury Chair Co., 652-658 6th NW
27. Macey Co., 940-1004 S. Division
28. Marvel Mfg Co., North and GR&I RR
29. Michigan Cabinet Co., 650 Front NW
30. Michigan Chair Co., 803 Godfrey SW
31. Michigan Desk Co., 334 Monroe NW
32. Mueller & Slack Co., 230-250 Monroe NW
33. Nachtegall Mfg. Co., 429-441 Front SW
34. National Seating Co., 40-50 Market NW
35. Nelson-Matter Furn. Co., 33-37 Monroe NW
36. Oriel Cabinet Co., 408 Monroe NW
37. C. S. Paine Co., 514 Butterworth SW
38. Phoenix Furn. Co., 25 Summer NW
39. Practical Sewing Cabinet, 317 Madison Ave SE
40. John D. Raab Chair Co., 840 Monroe NW
41. Retting Furn. Co., 901 Godfrey SW
42. Rex Mfg. Co., 18-20 Huron NW
43. C. B. Robinson & Sons, 6-8 Huron NW
44. Royal Furn. Co., 152-172 Monroe NW
45. Ryan Rattan Chair Co., 29 Ionia NW
46. Sligh Furn. Co., 201 Logan SW
47. G. S. Smith, 154-156 Kent NW
48. Snyder Furn. Co., 250 Ionia SW
49. Steel Furn. Co., 232-234 Front NW
50. Sterling Desk Co., 102-116 Prescott SW
51. Stickley Bros. Co., 837-861 Godfrey SW
52. Stow & Davis Furn. Co., 70-112 Front SW
53. Valley City Desk Co., 192 Butterworth SW
54. Veit Mfg. Co., 60-62 Coldbrook NW
55. Wagemaker Co., 454 Market SW
56. White-Steel Sanitary Furn. Co.,
    175 Mt Vernon NW
57. Widdicomb Furn Co., 650 Dewey NW
58. John Widdicomb Co., 601 5th NW
59. Wilmarth Show Case Co., 1544 Jefferson SE

④ *Berkey & Gay Plant No. 1* (GRPL, 78-1-15)

⑬ *Grand Rapids Chair Company* (GRPL, 78-1-82)

㉗ *Macey Company* (GRPL, 78-6-1)

(6) *Century Furniture Company* (GRPL, 78-6-1)

(18) *Gunn Furniture Company* (GRPL, 78-2-13.5)

(30) *Michigan Chair Company* (GRPL, 78-2-71.5)

(44) *Royal Furniture Company* (GRPL, 84-21-5)

38 *Phoenix Furniture Company* (GRPL, 91-2-9)

36 *Oriel Cabinet Company* (GRPL, 91-2-8)

(59) *Wilmarth Showcase Company* (GRPL, 84-21-5)

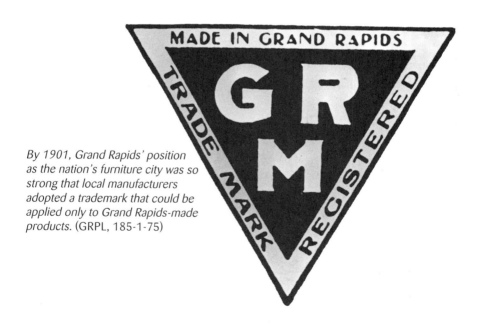

By 1901, Grand Rapids' position as the nation's furniture city was so strong that local manufacturers adopted a trademark that could be applied only to Grand Rapids-made products. (GRPL, 185-1-75)

Chapter 2

The City's Divided Workers: Religion, Property, and Ethnic Loyalties

While the Grand Rapids furniture men and their financier allies formed a tightly knit fraternity of mutual advantage, furniture factory workers were divided along fault lines of religion, class, and ethnicity. As the city's workforce grew, fed chiefly by immigration, these differences created a formidable barrier to collective action against entrenched economic interests. Language and social customs, together with clearly demarcated neighborhoods, distrust of those practicing the "wrong" religion, and continued hostilities based on old-country traditions produced fractures among workers in urban America. If German-Polish animosity existed in Europe, for example, it did not suddenly disappear on the other side of the Atlantic.[1]

In Grand Rapids as in other cities, immigrants tended to settle in enclaves where they could share extended family connections, speak their native language, and worship in neighborhood churches. But even within these tightly knit ethnic communities, old-world regional identities (were you from Poznan or Lublin? from Overisel or Friesland? Galicia or Lithuania?) and past loyalties shaped lives on and off the job and made it difficult for workers to organize and act collectively for any sustained time. Immigrants defined themselves in terms of home, family, neighborhood, and church — not as wage earners within a capitalist system.

Strength in Isolation

Dutch immigrants were among the first Europeans to come to West Michigan. They began arriving in the late 1840s, and by 1880 made up 71 percent of all foreign-born residents of Grand Rapids. By 1900, recent Dutch immigrants (those arriving since 1880), together with their predecessors and their children, accounted for more than one-quarter of the total population of Grand Rapids. Ten years later, at the height of the great wave of European immigration to American shores, one-third of the city's population was of Dutch birth or ancestry.[2]

While economic pressures in northern Europe, especially a profound agricultural depression in the 1880s, were crucial factors in the decision to emigrate, religious motives ranked high as well. In the years after 1859, the year Charles Darwin published his theory of evolution, the drive to rely less on traditional religious doctrine to guide public life grew among many political and economic leaders. The new urban and industrial life taking shape in Europe served to intensify the debate about whether or not the secular approach to solving political problems should take precedence over the older religious – or sacred – way of viewing the world.

In America, this debate took mainstream religious groups into the area of social reform, inspiring them to strive to clean up slums, attack child labor abuses, and campaign for universal temperance. Meanwhile, more conservative and fundamentalist groups stressed that church-based doctrine required the salvation of souls, not slums. In the Netherlands, certain that the rising tide of secular influences was corrupting their state church, disaffected, "God-fearing" Hollanders left home in pursuit of the opportunity to practice "pure" religion.

From the time of their earliest West Michigan settlement, the Dutch preferred cultural and ecclesiastical isolation. These new puritans felt that the greater the gulf that separated religious practice from "worldly concerns," the better it would be for their spiritual lives. The Dutch language was an important vehicle of worship and instruction. Not until 1902 was any concession made to church services in English, and not until 1910 was a Hollander newspaper published in English. As one prominent Dutch spokesman put it, "In our isolation is our strength."[3]

The Dutch community fought hard to keep itself distinct and apart from the urban industrial culture surrounding it. In the spring of 1888, the Grand Rapids Street Railway Company installed a new line that went past a Christian Reformed church, carrying passengers beyond the city's eastern limits to Reeds Lake, a popular spot for sports, picnics, and revelry. The members of the congregation were outraged, objecting to the noise of the steam-driven engines pulling the carriages, disrupting their Sunday church services, and claiming they feared danger to their children. More important, the strait-laced congregants detested the "common rowdyism and drunkenness prevalent among the merrymakers on the line on Sundays." When the company ignored their call to suspend the line's operation on their Sabbath, the men and women of the congregation repeatedly tore up the track in a running battle that went on for more than a month. Peace finally descended when the Kent County Circuit Court enjoined the company from running that particular line on Sunday.[4]

A second incident, far more severe, brought forth a rare censure from the municipal establishment. In June 1905, a smallpox epidemic swept through the city, killing 34 residents. The Dutch represented a high proportion of those infected, and the city physician and other health officers noted that the greatest opposition to vaccination had come from Dutch neighborhoods. Dr. Thomas M. Koon, the city health officer, found cases among the Dutch that had been hidden, including a man selling milk who was later stricken with the disease. Such episodes of public contact that sent contamination throughout the closely packed neighborhoods frightened people and raised the stakes of untreated or diseased carriers to new heights. "Every unvaccinated person," stated Dr. Koon, "is a menace to this city." In an attempt to curtail the dangers to public health, the city council passed an ordinance closing some public meeting places and limiting the operating hours of others, including churches.

The local Dutch churches protested the closures vigorously. Alderman Ate Dykstra introduced a resolution calling upon the Board of Health not to discriminate against the churches, especially those on the city's southeast side. This conflict between Dutch Reform Calvinism and the new urban environment was not soon forgotten by either the Dutch or government officials, especially since the epidemic had a direct cost to the city and county exceeding $20,000.[5]

"Little Hollands"

While not all Dutch immigrants became furniture workers, the majority of furniture workers were Dutch. At the turn of the century, when their numbers peaked, nearly half the 7,000-man labor force of the city's chief industry was drawn from these religiously cantankerous people.[6] The overwhelming majority of Dutch immigrants to Grand Rapids and West Michigan came from the provinces of Zeeland and Friesland. To outsiders, they were a cohesive group, indistinguishable from one another and allied in their purpose to remain wedded to the Reformed faith and the Dutch language. Nevertheless, regional disagreements separated the Dutch immigrants from many of the rest of the city's wage earners, and seemingly minor theological differences often divided them from each other.

Antagonistic relationships among various Dutch groups did not end when they left their native land, but persisted intact to Grand Rapids, where provincial differences were expressed and strengthened. Rather than cluster ghetto-fashion in a single "Little Holland," the Dutch settled in various pockets around the city, creating several "Little Hollands." In fact, to be entirely accurate, these Dutch enclaves could more appropriately be called "Little Zeeland," "Little Friesland," or "Little Overisel," after the various Netherlands locations of origin. The geographic dispersion of the Dutch into five distinct neighborhoods on both sides of the river served to reinforce old-country regional differences and inflame sectarian conflicts based on differing interpretations of Scripture.[7]

The earliest Dutch settlers in West Michigan aligned themselves with the Old Reformed Church in New York, which dated from 1628 and became known locally in 1867 as the Reformed Church in America (RCA). Later arrivals were alarmed by the Reformed Church's "worldly" perspectives and seceded to form the Christian Reformed Church (CRC) in 1857. During the 1880s, the RCA's sanctioning of secular fraternities such as the Freemasons and acceptance of their members as church members, its support of public education, and its willingness to hold open discussions on the legitimacy of labor unions provoked charges that it had dallied too readily with the concerns of this world and not the next. Dissenters feared that such accommodations to secular society would undermine the strict Calvinist heritage they had come to America to preserve and perpetuate.[8]

Increasingly Americanized attitudes coupled with theological differences that centered on hymns, revivals, and prayer meetings produced a series of eruptions and secessions and further fragmentation of local Calvinist churches. In the years between 1882 and 1890, for example, the Fourth Reformed Church in the city's Fifth Ward was torn by schism. The Coldbrook Street Church congregation repeatedly sought injunctions from the Kent County Circuit Court for a cease and desist order to prevent seizure of church property by "renegade churchmen."[9] Such antagonism was reinforced by provincial differences, and the situation showed little sign of improving over time. As late as 1924, the Holland classis pronounced, "We are convinced that ecclesiastical alliances of any kind between orthodox and liberal are contrary to the word of God."

The Polish Community

Polish immigrants began to join the furniture industry workforce in significant numbers just as migration from the Netherlands was slowing. Like the Dutch, the Poles possessed old-country provincial loyalties. From the 1850s to around 1870, most of Grand Rapids' relatively small Polish immigrant population came from Posen and other provinces in Prussian-occupied Poland. Beginning in 1870, an influx from the eastern or Russian sector of the divided country increased their numbers.[10] The majority of the Polish newcomers clustered on the West Side, buying homes and raising families across the Grand River from most of the city's Dutch population. A second, smaller Polish settlement grew up on the East Side, in the area around today's Michigan Street and Eastern Avenue that was called the Brickyard because of its proximity to a number of brickworks. By 1909, of the city's 110,000 residents, almost a tenth were Polish. Although they were a much smaller portion of the total population than the Dutch, Poles made up slightly more than 40 percent of the furniture factory workforce. Together, Dutch and Polish workers accounted for four-fifths of the total furniture workforce, with most of the remaining fifth coming from Scandinavia, Lithuania, and Italy.[11]

Their Catholic faith made the Poles stand out in a predominantly Protestant city. But they did not find a close and comforting embrace among the German and Irish Catholic groups who had preceded them to Grand Rapids. Many Germans had risen through the ranks to hold the skilled jobs in the furniture factories, becoming foremen and shop directors in the new industrial setting, supervising both Dutch and Polish immigrant wage earners. Germans also dominated the local Catholic Church structure, a reminder to the Poles that just as their native country had been absorbed into the German empire, so, too, were they required to defer to their German co-religionists in spiritual matters.

Parish politics were emblematic of the friction caused by Polish subordination to the Germans in the workforce and the church. During their early years in Grand Rapids, the German-speaking Poles who had emigrated from Posen in Prussian Poland joined the local German community to worship at St. Mary's Catholic Church. By 1880, they had enough money to purchase two lots and begin building their own church on the West Side at the corner of Davis Street and Fourth Avenue. The new parish was dedicated in May 1882, shortly after the diocese of Grand Rapids was established under the leadership of Bishop Henry Joseph Richter, formerly of Cincinnati.[12]

The dream of the Poles was to recreate in their new homeland a church modeled on the Basilica at Trezenieszno in Posen, but it fell to the recently appointed bishop to provide a namesake for the new edifice and parish. Seeking a patron saint whose legacy appealed chiefly to the Germans but nonetheless acknowledged a strong Polish connection as well, the German-born Bishop Richter chose St. Adalbert and, in so doing, conveyed the double-edged relationship between the episcopate and his charges. St. Adalbert, a German monk, had brought Christianity to the Poles at sword point in the ninth century in the wake of a German invasion. His shrine in Gniezno stood in the heart of eastern Poland, in the region between Poznan and Trzmeszno from which many of the city's West Side immigrants had come.

More than a decade later, the Polish Brickyard community on the East Side established the city's second Polish parish. Over the objections of the parishioners, who wanted to name their church after the Polish St. Stanislaus, Richter issued a decree dedicating the structure to the German St. Isidore.[13] Both names, St. Adalbert and St. Isidore, underscored the Poles' second place in the city's immigrant social and economic hierarchy.

Richter acted again in 1904 to maintain discipline in his diocese and preserve its distinctly German flavor when he transferred Father Simon Ponganis out of Grand Rapids to the distant Siberia of Gaylord, Michigan. Ponganis had been the first Polish priest in the Grand Rapids parish, arriving in 1886, five years after Richter. He served St. Adalbert's well, but his attempts to promote the movement for a Polish National Church in the United States not only brought him into personal conflict with the German bishop, but also served as a direct challenge to the established national ecclesiastical structure dominated by Germans and Irish. Ponganis also troubled Richter by urging Poles to act collectively to assert their political influence. The Polish Political Club that he founded in 1899 began to mobilize immigrant voters, electing a Polish alderman the year before Ponganis's departure and helping to elect George Ellis mayor in 1906.[14]

Unshared Experiences

Aside from the taunts and occasional clashes between groups of young boys, there is little evidence of any strong antagonism between Poles and Dutch in the city. In fact, there was apparently less friction between Catholic and Calvinist than between the Dutch Reformed and their American Protestant counterparts. Neither, however, were there signs of close cooperation. Although class might have been a common denominator, the two immigrant groups remained separated by language and religion, a division magnified by the wages they earned and their household circumstances. There was little ground of shared experiences outside the workplace, and even at work their interaction was limited. Residential patterns established by 1911 suggested that each group felt most comfortable within its own "territory," leaving the fragmented immigrant community scant basis for class cohesion.

The principal reason for the persistent differences was time of arrival into the city. The Dutch had arrived earlier and been in the factories longer, giving them an economic advantage when it came to wages. On a weekly basis, Netherlanders earned about 8 percent more than their Polish counterparts. Yearly totals demonstrated a slightly larger gap between the two sets of wage earners, suggesting Dutch workers were not only paid more, but also received more hours of work. At the end of the year, Dutch immigrants took home an average of $559, compared with the Polish annual average of $511, a difference of nearly 10 percent.

Immigrant wages were conditioned in part by the degree to which the workers had some salable skill: language, literacy, knowledge of arithmetic. As workers gained more of these skills, they made a slow climb up the wage scale and, supplemented by income from other family members, gathered the resources needed to acquire property. It was not a meteoric rise, but one that came over a long period of time. Second-generation Dutch tended not to remain in the furniture factories, but those who did earned a higher wage, about $646 a year, nearly $90 or 14 per cent more than their first-generation counterparts. Second-generation Germans and Swedes were more likely to remain in the industrial shops, rising to positions as foremen and managers and commanding higher wages – about $700 a year – than the second-generation Dutch.[15]

The wage differences at the factories carried over into individual households and had a direct bearing on the ways in which Dutch and Polish families supplemented the primary breadwinner's income. By 1910, Dutch households were larger, averaging five children as compared with the Polish average of two. The children of the Dutch workers were older and as a consequence were more likely to work outside the home. The contributions of these older children, especially the males, accounted for 40 percent of all additional income brought into Dutch households.[16]

Among Polish immigrant families, children working outside the home added barely one-fourth of the supplemental income. The greatest portion of additional money came from boarders and lodgers, usually other Poles or the growing numbers of Lithuanians who began making their way to Grand Rapids late in the nineteenth century. Two-thirds of the city's Polish families supplemented their furniture factory income by taking in boarders. One-third of the families derived more than half their household income from boarders.

Household conditions for Polish immigrants were also shaped by the fact that their homes or flats were consistently smaller and therefore more crowded than those of their Dutch coworkers. Polish households had twice as many people sleeping per room and more rooms used for sleeping than was common for either first- or second-generation Netherlands immigrants.[17]

The Property Trap

The need for supplemental income in immigrant households arose from the fact that more than half the Polish wage earners and nearly three-quarters of the Dutch workers owned their own homes and needed additional income to pay off loans and mortgages.[18] Although Grand Rapids boosters pointed with pride to the fact that the Furniture City claimed the nation's highest rate of home ownership among medium-sized cities, their claim told only part of the story. The majority of homes in Grand Rapids, especially among the furniture workers, were small, inexpensive, and heavily mortgaged, and Polish immigrants were the city's most heavily indebted homeowners. [19]

Nor were the homeowners evenly distributed around the city. The areas with the highest incidence of home ownership were the predominantly Polish West Side, hugging the area between the railroad tracks near the river and the steep bluffs rising up along the westernmost city limits, and the Dutch East Side vicinity of the Brickyard, in the Second and Fourth wards.

Because the energies devoted to home ownership gave immigrants some "marginal control over their social and economic environment," the high rate of home ownership among them represented an effort to solidify their "precarious economic status." Home ownership provided an edge against the caprices of landlords and the threat of eviction in the days before tenants' rights existed, and it offered promise for the future. Owning even the tiniest home motivated families to persevere in their efforts to leave a tangible legacy for the next generation.[20]

For many Dutch and Polish factory workers, the investments in their homes represented an enormous financial stake, especially as they struggled to meet mortgage payments, pay property taxes, and make repairs and improvements to their property. With too much money invested to pull out and too little cash to exercise political influence, working-class homeowners found themselves in an enticing "property trap." They were caught in an arrangement of dependence upon their employers who were both their source of income and, through their banks, the holders of their home loans.[21]

In 1912 the National Housing Association, a pioneer organization devoted to urban planning and housing reform, sponsored a symposium on worker home ownership that took place in Philadelphia. Several speakers praised the idea of widespread private home buying as promoting "stability" and "social responsibility" among working families, while others pointed to the precarious position into which home ownership forced wage earners. "A working man owning his home, which is purchased after many years of savings," argued one participant, "puts himself to some extent in the hands of such employers as are most convenient for him to get to for further employment." Indeed, continued the same speaker, a wage earner must remember "that if he buys his home and gets it half paid for, it is likely, as in the case of a strike, pressure may be brought to bear which will prevent him from getting a raise in wage or betterment of conditions."[22]

High interest and mortgage rates represented another dimension of the property trap, especially in Grand Rapids where most workingmen's mortgages were from banks controlled by the factory owners. Interest rates hovered at 6 percent, relatively high considering that a savings account returned 2 to 3 percent in a bank or 3 to 4 percent in a savings and loan. Also problematic was the fact that mortgages were short term and had to be paid off or renewed every one to three years.

Additionally, a large number of homes were assessed below the national average. In the early decades of the twentieth century, Grand Rapids workers were putting a great deal of money into homes that yielded less value than similar structures around the United States. Almost one-third (29 percent) of all the mortgaged homes in Grand Rapids fell into the under-$2,500 category; the only other city approaching such a high proportion of low-valued homes was another industrial city, Scranton, Pennsylvania. In Grand Rapids, these very modest, single-family homes, nearly 3,000 in number, were small, generally built of wood or, occasionally, cinder block, and perched on lots measuring 50' x 50' or less. Valued at an average of $1,174, they carried an average debt of $872 – about 1.5 times as much as the average Dutch immigrant furniture worker earned annually and nearly 1.75 times the yearly income of a Polish wage earner. Collectively, this group of householders labored under an average debt/value ratio of 49.2 percent.[23] In plain English, those least able to afford a home owed more money in relation to the value of their homes than homeowners in either the city or the nation.

Another 4,000 or so Grand Rapids wage earners owned single-family homes in the $2,500 to $5,000 range, with an average value of $3,325 and a typical debt of $1,439. Although their mortgages were considerably higher than those on the financial rung below them, their lower debt/value ratio, of 43.3 percent, represented a somewhat lesser degree of dependence on borrowed money. Nevertheless, for both groups of homeowners, these small, heavily encumbered homes were a major financial burden, especially in light of the erratic nature of the early twentieth-century economy and the lack of unemployment insurance or bargaining power among workers.[24]

While home ownership to some individuals represented a powerful symbol of the "American Dream," a material statement of possessing something solid and substantial, the reality was often more fleeting and uncertain. Employment in the highly unpredictable furniture industry brought no guarantee of income year after year, and the ability to repay sizable home mortgage loans could readily vanish in any of the frequent national cyclical downturns in the years after 1890. Surviving the depression of 1893-96 still left the debt-ridden homeowner to confront the Panic of 1906-07 and the protracted recessions of 1910-11 and 1913-14. Nor were these homes, bought so dearly and held so tenuously, particularly valuable on the open market. In terms of a logical investment of time and money, home ownership was not always a wise economic decision.

Residential Patterns

The burden of property spanned the river, the hilltops, and the ravines of Grand Rapids, and almost every element of the wage-earning population was affected by a high level of mortgage indebtedness, which was one of the unifying threads among the city's various ethnic and religious groups. But the fellowship of encumbered indebtedness did not always bring with it equality of living conditions, and distinct differences in occupational and propertied lifestyles characterized the city's neighborhoods.

Far above the ordinary worker's aspirations were the hilltop precincts where the city's elite lived. Here, in the neighborhood today known as Heritage Hill, bankers, factory owners, lawyers, and other men of wealth and substance occupied the most expensive homes in the city. In this exclusive area, spanning the Second, Third and Tenth wards, lived several furniture men John Widdicomb, John Mowat, William Gay, and Robert Irwin. Nearby were the Fountain Street Baptist Church and the equally prestigious Park Congregational Church. Broad, tree-lined streets boasted solid brick houses built on sizable lots of 150' x 100' and more. Private carriages and, later, automobiles carried residents downtown for work, shopping, or to the Peninsular Club for a convivial mixture of business, politics, and dining.

Directly to the north, in the Fourth and Fifth wards, were the frame homes of the working classes. This North End neighborhood of private, one-family homes housed a variety of blue-collar wage earners, mostly emigrants from New England and New York, with a number of Canadian and British immigrants mixed in. The area did not grow as quickly as the West Side or the southeastern portions of Grand Rapids, nor did it promise rapid growth. Rather, much of the area remained unplatted open land, far enough from the factories that it inspired little but speculation in small lots. Property values fell into the lower half of all homes in the city, and apartment houses, boarding rooms, and flats played little part in the residential geography.[25]

Directly to the south of the hilltop precincts stretched the area along Madison Avenue, where the predominantly professional, native Protestant population gradually gave way to a neighborhood of second-generation Dutch who found work in a variety of clerical positions or small independent jobs. Primarily skilled craftsmen and retail shop owners lived here, and only towards the southernmost reaches of the Madison Avenue neighborhood did wage earners appear. An interesting feature of this area was the limited number of small consumer services such as groceries, drugstores, or restaurants. Neighborhood residents, even if they did not own cars, could shop downtown or along busy Franklin Street thanks to their own mobility and to the proximity to the streetcar lines that enhanced the desirability of the neighborhood.

On either side of the Grand River were two immigrant neighborhoods populated largely by furniture workers. A strongly working-class community of Dutch grew up along Grandville Avenue to the southwest, and large numbers of Polish immigrants chose to make their homes along Davis Avenue on the west side of the river. Unlike the leafier, more spacious Madison Avenue area, these neighborhoods were among the most congested in the city.[26]

The rates of home ownership in these two predominantly immigrant areas were slightly above the city average, but the size of the homes, the lots they stood on, and their value fell far below the city average. Whereas properties on Madison Avenue might be as large as 80' x 100', lots in the Dutch and Polish neighborhoods seldom exceeded 360 square feet. Based on an analysis of tax records, the average $1,620 value of these working-class homes placed them among the poorest third of the city.

Like Madison Avenue, Grandville Avenue had a trolley line. Part of the interurban system of western Michigan, the Grandville Avenue line carried business traffic, local shoppers, and workers on their way to and from the furniture factories, the Pére Marquette railroad yards, and the other large industrial plants situated along the route. Because it sat on a relatively high prominence separated from the rest of the city by steep ravines, the Grandville neighborhood served to promote the self-imposed isolation of many of its Dutch Reformed residents. A large number of groceries, drugstores, and butcher shops helped to make the area nearly independent, fostering a community that was "in Grand Rapids" without necessarily being "of Grand Rapids."

Further to the north, Davis Avenue, by contrast, lacked streetcars. Homes in this neighborhood were either the usual small frame or cinder block structures typical of other working-class areas, built on lots that had been held for speculation by several of the city's leading citizens.[27] The homes stood crowded together, providing cramped quarters for families who took in boarders to supplement income from wages.

The average value of homes in this part of Grand Rapids was $800, among the lowest 20 percent of the city's assessed housing. Residents included a high concentration of general laborers, finishers, and varnishers whose working lives centered on the furniture factories. There were few grocery stores, meat markets, or other service businesses, and residents had to travel to find places for food and drink. The only businesses conveniently located here were the railroad lines and furniture factories.

Dutch and Polish lived side by side in the East Side neighborhood known as the Brickyard, and nearby brickworks provided employment for large numbers of residents. Like other immigrant neighborhoods, the Brickyard was crowded, with three alleys, one narrow street, and 103 families clustered together on more than 100 lots that averaged 800 square feet. Eventually, the Brickyard grew into a community of 1,000 Polish families.[28]

"What's the Matter With Grand Rapids?"

In an era that saw workers throughout the United States organizing collectively in an effort to shift the balance of power away from those who seemed to hold all the economic cards, the furniture workers of Grand Rapids seemed content with the status quo. Not until 1911 did they stage a citywide strike to protest wages and working conditions, and even then, they ended up capitulating to the owners without gaining a single concession.

During the strike, William "Big Bill" Haywood, cofounder of the Industrial Workers of the World (IWW), the most radical labor union organization in modern American history, paid a visit to Grand Rapids. Two years later, the IWW's official organ in the eastern United States published an editorial signed with the pseudonym O.L. Wakeup (Organized Labor Wake Up). Possibly authored by Haywood and titled "What's the Matter With Grand Rapids?" the piece attempted to explain why so many workers had failed in their efforts to challenge the city's industrial leadership. The analysis cited three critical factors: ethnic divisions, both between and within various immigrant groups; adherence to organized religion; and a high rate of home ownership among wage earners.

These three factors assured that the city would continue to be ruled by its factory owners and financiers. The wage earners themselves made it easy. With their large families, costly mortgages, and heavy responsibilities, they were tied to a conservative, propertied, church-oriented existence that all but extinguished union activity in the Furniture City. The allegiance to owning a home and "getting ahead" for oneself and one's family, argued the editorial, obscured the real task of challenging the entire capitalist system. How could a worker confront his employer and demand economic justice, he argued, if the need for mortgage payments and home improvements lurked behind every paycheck?

The editorial's author saw home ownership as a chief cause of the "conservative and timid" nature of the working man, and "a snare and delusion for the workers." He claimed that in his 24 years of travel in the United States, "I have always observed that those cities in which large numbers of workers owned their homes were always low-wage, long-workday, open-shop towns." Even if wages had been adequate, he argued, the costs of maintaining a house – taxes, assessments, insurance, repairs – only furthered the sense of dependency. Once on the "home-buying stint," he wrote, all extra time and money found its way into the home. "You can't help it, that is the home-buying psychology." The editorial extolled the thirty or so pioneer members of Grand Rapids IWW Local 202 and damned the thousands of other "wishy-washy" trade unionist advocates in the city. This tirade reflected not only disappointment with the workers of Grand Rapids, but also the deep division among labor organizers that handicapped any attempt to promote a broadly based action in the workplace.[29]

Yet were the city's working classes really all that passive and were employers quite so powerful? Certainly ethnic and religious divisions inhibited a sustained class-conscious movement, but in the short-term battle that took place in 1911, wage earners demonstrated they were able to assert more unity and control over their numbers than the editorial writer and others anticipated.

Endnotes

1. Several authors have written about class-consciousness in America. See, for example: Louis Hartz, *The Liberal Tradition in America* (New York: Harcourt, Brace & World, 1955); Daniel Boorstin, *The Genius of American Politics* (Chicago: University of Chicago Press, 1953); Stephen Thernstrom, *Poverty and Progress* (Cambridge: Harvard University Press, 1964); Jeremy Brecher, *Strike* (Boston: South End Press, 1977); David Brody, *Steelworkers in America: The Nonunion Era* (New York: Harper Torchbooks, 1960); John Bodnar, *The Transplanted* (Bloomington: Indiana University Press, 1985); For a fuller view of the literature on class- consciousness in the United States since the turn of the century, see Aileen Kraditor, *The Radical Persuasion: 1890-1917* (Baton Rouge: Louisiana State University Press, 1981).
2. Robert F. Swierenga, "The Dutch in West Michigan: The Impact of a Contractual Community," *Grand River Valley History,* Vol. 18, 2001, p. 18.
3. David G. Vanderstel, "The Dutch of Grand Rapids, Michigan 1848-1900: Immigrant Neighborhoods and Community Development in a Nineteenth-Century City," (unpublished Ph.D. dissertation, Kent State University, 1983); The most complete research on the Dutch Reformed Church in the Progressive Era was done by Henry Zwaanstra, *Reformed Thought and Experience in a New World* (Amsterdam: J. H. Kok, 1973), and James D. Bratt, *Dutch Calvinism in Modern America: A History of a Conservative Subculture* (Grand Rapids: William B. Eerdmans Publishing Company, 1984). An older work, less detailed but nonetheless valuable, is John Kromminga, *The Christian Reformed Church: A Study in Orthodoxy* (Grand Rapids: Baker Book House, 1949).
4. Vanderstel, p. 470; Z. Z. Lydens, *The Story of Grand Rapids* (Grand Rapids, 1966), p. 133.
5. *Civic News,* June 17, 1905, pp. 3, 6.
6. *Report of the Immigration Commission* (Washington, D.C., 1911) p. 480.
7. Vanderstel, p. 410.
8. Swierenga, p. 20.
9. Vanderstel, pp. 466, 514; Kromminga, pp. 104-5.

10. Eduard Adam Skendzel, "The Polanders," *Grand River Valley Review,* Vol. IV, No. 2, Spring/Summer 1983, p. 3.
11. *Report of the Immigration Commission* (1911) p. 480.
12. John McGee, T*he Catholic Church in the Grand River Valley* (Grand Rapids: St. Andrews Cathedral, 1950).
13. Skendzel, "Polonian Musings," (photocopied typescript in the Grand Rapids History and Special Collections Center, Grand Rapids Public Library), v. 2, pp. 406-10; Harold Abramson, "Ethnic Diversity Within Catholicism," *Journal of Social History* 4 (1971), pp. 359-488.
14. The struggle between Richter and Ponganis symbolized the larger stresses within the Catholic Church as it confronted the diverse waves of immigrants after 1880, especially when complicated by the growth of nationalism among many eastern Europeans. For a detailed case study, see Victor Greene, *For God and Country: The Rise of Polish and Lithuanian Ethnic Consciousness in America 1860-1910* (Madison: State Historical Society of Wisconsin, 1975) pp. 122-142; Skendzel, "Musings," p. 410.
15. *Report of the Immigration Commission* (1911) p. 493, table 25, p. 500.
16. Ibid. pp. 502-3, tables 34, 38.
17. Ibid. p. 493, table 25, 500-3, tables 21, 34, 38.
18. Ibid. p. 531.
19. Bureau of Census, *Mortgage Report;* Herbert B. Dorau and Albert G. Hinman, *Urban Land Economics* (New York: Macmillan, 1928).
20. Carolyn Kirk and Gordon Kirk, "Impact of the City on Home Ownership," *Journal of Urban History* 7 (August 1981), p. 473.
21. Zunz, *The Changing Face of Inequality,* see Chapter VI, "Neighborhoods, Homes and the Dual Housing Market," pp. 129-76; This idea has been developed more fully with its political implications by Michael E. Stone, "Housing, Mortgage Lending and the Contradictions of Capitalism," in Tabb and Sawers, *Marxism and the Metropolis,* pp. 179-207; Matthew Edel, et al, chapters 4 and 5, pp. 134-94.
22. National Housing Association, *Housing Problems in America* (Cambridge: Harvard University Press, 1913), v. 2, p. 283.
23. Bureau of Census, *Mortgage Report.*
24. Ibid.
25. City directory listings of all apartments, flats, boarding houses and lodgings, and hotels for 1911, *Grand Rapids City Directory,* 1912.
26. Federal Census 1910, v. 2, p. 954, table V.
27. See city tax records for 1909-12, ward 6, book 2, pp. 665-67.
28. Vanderstel, p. 410; *Immigration Commission,* v. 15, p. 513; Skendzel, "The Polanders," p. 4.
29. *Solidarity,* October 4, 1913, p. 1. For a more complete description of the Industrial Workers of the World's efforts to organize skilled workers across America, see Melvin Dubovsky, *We Shall Be All: A History of the Industrial Workers of the World* (Champagne-Urbana: University of Illinois Press, 1988).

Inside the Furniture Factories

Shortly after the 1911 furniture strike, a photographer toured the John Widdicomb Company and several other Grand Rapids furniture companies, recording working conditions and men at work in a variety of departments. In nearly every case, the machinery lacked safety guards. In order to gain adequate lighting, detailed work such as assembling, carving, and decorating was arranged in front of large windows around the perimeter of the room.

Routers, unidentified factory (GRPL, 84-21-11)

*Decorating department,
John Widdicomb Company*
(GRPL, 54-48-2)

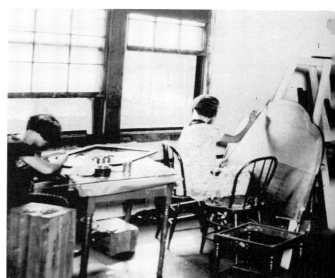

Assembling tables, Phoenix Furniture Company (GRPL, 54-41-3)

Carving department, John Widdicomb Company (GRPL, 54-48-2)

Veneer-laying department, John Widdicomb Company (GRPL, 54-48-2)

Machine department, John Widdicomb Company (GRPL, 54-48-2)

Rip saws, John Widdicomb Company (GRPL, 54-48-2)

Chapter 3

Leadership in Transition:
Selecting Mayor and Minister

The 1906 mayoral election changed Grand Rapids' political landscape as two widely different groups battled for command of City Hall. On one side was a conservative coalition led by furniture manufacturers and bankers determined to assert political control over the city in order to hold tight to the reins of economic power. On the other side stood various groups of ethnic and working-class voters, equally determined to use their superior numbers to gain political power. Both groups were intent on wresting control of the municipal government from the middle-class officials they held accountable for a series of frauds and corrupt practices.

The importance of the contest rested on the fact that in a democratic political system the majority of votes cast carries the day, and the greater majority of wage-dependent workers would always outnumber the fewer men of wealth. Although the employers may have had overwhelming influence at the factory, it was the workers who had the last word at the ballot box. The industrialists had to develop a popular agenda and find a way to offset the working-class voters' majority.[1]

City Scandals

The confrontation between employers and wage earners at the ballot box had its first test of strength in 1900 when the governing leadership was discredited in a scandal that created a chance for new political figures to emerge. An infamous fraud, known as the water scandal, was perpetrated on the people of Grand Rapids with the complicity of their elected leaders. The scandal involved officials at every level, including Mayor George Perry, City Attorney Lant K. Salsbury, the city clerk and 16 of 24 aldermen, as well as three newspaper editors and at least one elected state official.

The water scandal began when the city issued municipal bonds, essentially a loan to be repaid with taxpayer dollars, for construction of a pipeline and water treatment plant to supply Lake Michigan water to Grand Rapids. The trouble was that the bonds were issued for an amount far greater than the actual cost of the project, with the difference to be shared among the various culprits. The Associated Press eventually blew the whistle on the plot, and a handful of honest officials pressed for punishment. Eventually exposed in newspaper stories and probed by a grand jury, the guilty parties retired in disgrace, but not to jail.[2]

What the water scandal made clear was that those entrusted with guarding the city's best interests had failed. Tempted by ready access to loosely monitored city funds, they had engaged in a series of petty financial irregularities involving city funds in the years before the water scandal. Later, questions were raised about the handling of emergency procedures and relief efforts during the Grand River's worst-ever recorded flood in 1904. By then, the cry for reform was in the air.

The Grand Rapids Good Government League

Despite their economic strength and cohesion in business matters, the furniture manufacturers and their banker allies had not been able to move into positions of political power. They could elect members of the city council from their own wards because they dominated those neighborhoods, but they lacked sufficient organization and clout to move into citywide offices.

The industrialists and the financiers found it difficult to agree upon a single approach as a political force, and the vagaries of local issues created no clearly defined agenda. They were inexperienced and naive about the give and take of ward-level politics, unable to organize drives for voter registration and unwilling to reach effectively into all areas of the city by such tactics as visiting pool halls and saloons in search of support. More important, they lacked centralized leadership and a strong party organization. Rather, they relied on the Grand Rapids Good Government League, more an association of like-minded moralists than a disciplined vehicle to achieve political power.

The Good Government League, founded in 1906 and made up mostly of lawyers, businessmen, and industrialists living in the hilltop neighborhood, focused on moral corruption. Of utmost importance was the saloon issue. For years league members worked to introduce zoning ordinances that would create special corridors for the beer halls patronized by the working classes. This would have concentrated the saloons into smaller, more easily patrolled areas, and reduced the number of locations available. As a result, competition for the few authorized spots would drive up rental charges and increase the cost of doing business.

The saloon issue typified the league's approach to political problem solving. Clearly, no one among the city's residents advocated drunken brawls and fistfights, and support for the proposed regulation might conceivably have been found among diverse elements of the population who shared a desire for peace and orderly conduct. But rather than work towards a compromise solution in the city council, the league offered heavy-handed moralizing combined with demands for permanent changes that promised to bring order at the expense of pleasure. For these reformers, driving up the cost of doing beer-hall business was the first step to driving the saloons out of town.[3]

"Deacon" Ellis

In contrast to the Good Government League, the Republican Party of Michigan stood at the height of its organizational strength. Thanks to the adroit use of patronage by U.S. Senator James McMillan, Michigan's Republican Party secured a variety of offices from governor on down.[4] In western Michigan, Republican efforts helped elect William Alden Smith to the U.S. House and then the Senate. In 1906, to assure himself and his party uncritical support, Smith purchased the Grand Rapids *Herald* and within a short time elevated city hall beat reporter Arthur Vandenberg to the position of editor. The *Herald* gave its stamp of approval to the Republican mayoral candidate that year, George Ellis, who had won a seat in the State House of Representatives in 1904.

Although Ellis, like many successful Republican business leaders, had come to Grand Rapids early in his professional career, he always remained an outsider. Part of the reason was social; part was economic. Although Ellis was financially comfortable and occupied one of the more expensive homes in the city, the source of his money and the character of his leisure-time associations skirted the bounds of respectability. To the lawyers, merchants, and manufacturers who were his neighbors, Ellis, whose personal abstention from alcohol and tobacco had earned him the sobriquet "Deacon," was a dealmaker who never rose above the politics of smoke-filled back rooms.[5]

Reformers focused on Ellis's primary source of income, a series of storefront operations that he and his supporters claimed was a stock and grain brokerage business. His local detractors, along with the Chicago Board of Trade and the Illinois State Supreme Court, argued that Ellis operated a "bucket shop" or the commodities equivalent of a bookmaking operation. The bucket-shop operation was simple enough. Outside several "brokerage" offices operated by Ellis were posted the daily prices of various commodities such as oats, corn, and wheat. The customer wishing to play the market put forward his bid "on margin" to Ellis and waited for the change in price by a given future date. In theory, these transactions were no different from the operations of a legitimate commodities broker, except that no actual orders left for the Commodities Exchange in Chicago. Nor was possession of the commodities ever taken. Rather, the anticipated gains or resultant losses were settled between the "speculator" and his "broker" within the confines of the office.

In the public mind, the bucket-shop operations were synonymous with gambling, which they were, with Ellis "making book" on commodities futures just as off-track betting parlors make book on horse races today. Courtesy of Ellis, the ordinary man in the street could bet on the future prices of corn, wheat, and other commodities – without entering the "Pit" in Chicago – and play with the big-time speculators. Ellis and his defenders argued that the put-and-call transactions of these storefront operations allowed the small-time speculator in commodities to stake a claim on the exclusive world of the wealthy investor.

His detractors, however, claimed that Ellis knowingly engaged in fraud. League members called him guilty of "duping" the ignorant public into thinking their chances for gain were much greater than they really were, and the Chicago Board of Trade charged him with the unauthorized use of private services by tapping into telegraph lines that carried commodities information. In short, the civic reformers had a basis for calling Ellis a liar, a cheat, and a scoundrel, while those who "invested" in commodities at his shops still saw him as a man of the people.[6]

There is no evidence that his customers felt resentment towards Ellis. On the contrary, he gave a man with a few dollars to burn something other than cards or dice, something perhaps more "ritzy" that could dominate discussion in the corner tavern. Workingmen might sit over a few beers and talk about the beating they had taken in the market even as the city's elite gathered at the Peninsular Club and shared their own stories of gains or losses on the commodities exchange.

Ellis's political opponents claimed that he exploited misguided wage earners, separating honest workers from their money. They also raised the specter of Ellis's endorsement and sponsorship of such unwholesome sporting activities as baseball. He had helped organize the Western Baseball League in 1894, operating the Grand Rapids team franchise. Earlier, he had been a dominant force in forming the Atlantic Baseball League and served at the helm of its Newark, New Jersey, franchise for two years.[7]

To his detractors this was more proof of Ellis's rubbing elbows with the city's worst elements. They charged that baseball lured roughnecks and lowlifes to fields where drinking, cursing, and gambling took place openly. Sandlot baseball might be a proper diversion for children, but "professional" baseball's appeal to unrefined elements reinforced arguments about Ellis's moral standing. Not only was the conduct of spectators and players a moral issue, but the practice of playing Sunday games lent another volatile aspect to the political mix.

The *Civic News*

By 1906, Ellis's involvement in bucket shops and baseball drew critical articles and editorials from the *Civic News,* the official paper of the Grand Rapids Good Government League, which thundered against his attempts to run for mayor. "There is no reason," ran a story on page one, "why a city in its right mind should add another daub to its smirched reputation." A man such as he, who has never "turned his hand to honest labor or engaged in a productive business, is no friend of the working man," warned the *News*. With a final blast, the trumpet of civic pride appealed to every lover of "decency and order" not to support a thief.

Editorials in the daily newspapers criticizing Ellis paled in comparison to the vindictive rhetoric of the *Civic News*. Not content with merely striving to bring about changes in local government, the Good Government League joined forces with the Detroit Reform League in a statewide effort to promote reform. Eventually, local opposition to Ellis became associated with a campaign to eliminate perceived political undesirables statewide.

The *Civic News* lobbed its righteous anger at Ellis in a special issue prior to the April 1906 mayoral election. Ignoring the popularity that had brought him to a seat in the State House of Representatives in 1904 and his close ties with State Representative Gerritt Diekema and U.S. Senator William Alden Smith, the *News* listed reason after reason for not electing Ellis mayor. The paper depicted him as a morally challenged human being. "Practically every dollar of his fortune is 'tainted money' representing, as it does, the sufferings of little children and the agony of despairing women." Once in power, said the *News,* he would lure the children into gambling, speculation, and betting. These self-same children, with Ellis as their model, would then think it fine for a college-educated man, one smarter than most, to get rich by "preying upon the weaknesses of his fellow man."[8]

The Campaign

Rather than responding in kind, Ellis kept his eye on the prize. He accepted the argument that the time had come for reform, but argued it was wealthy special interests that were the problem. Voters needed to decide whether government should be controlled by the "people or the special interests." In his mind the "people" were the wage earners, his bucket-shop clientele, and baseball fans. In the "special interests" column were industrialists and economic development boosters. When he spoke, Ellis made it plain that his support of the common man was based on keeping the power of the wealthy in line with their numbers and limiting their economic influence.[9]

Ellis's appeal went beyond local concerns to embrace the larger issue of working-class politics. At the start of his campaign, Ellis outlined four major charges against the special interests. First, they had corrupted the government by demanding and receiving preferential tax assessments and, as a result, paying unfairly low property taxes. Second, special interests wielded undue influence at City Hall. Appointments to city service boards came to men who would never be chosen if filling those positions were "left to the people." Third, industrialists had overdeveloped riverfront property, especially on the West Side, rendering the river channel that flowed through the heart of the city narrow and susceptible to easy flooding, and threatening life and property in pursuit of profit. Finally, the liquor laws were enforced unequally, discriminating against the poor man's saloon without troubling upper-class private clubs.[10]

Ellis's claim that some individuals and businesses received preferential treatment at the hands of city tax assessors was not an idle charge. Physical expansion of the city was obvious to anybody who bothered to look. But the growth had not been evenly distributed, either in terms of industrial development or residential property. Boom-like growth had taken place in the already prosperous East Side Second Ward and, to a lesser degree, in the neighboring Third Ward, followed by gains in the promising Tenth and Eleventh wards. Conversely, the entire West Side had made only modest advances in the appreciation of property values, and growth and values actually declined in the northeastern Fifth Ward.[11]

Not only did it appear that the rich were getting away with lower taxes, but in an era before zoning ordinances, high assessments served as a means of preventing industrial development in residential areas. While underassessment of other locations acted to depress residential development in favor of industrial expansion, prime residential property on the Southeast Side would never be priced to attract new industrial plants. But the low property values in the Fifth Ward on the North End and the entire West Side made these working-class neighborhoods logical investment points for those interested in low-priced property for plant expansion. Low property values and the lack of zoning restrictions also made it possible to build factories in the same neighborhoods where workers lived.

Ellis's call for greater government control over development along the west bank of the Grand River and better flood control brought great support from the West Side. The issue of excessive riverfront development was directly tied to flood control, which had been on the minds of West Side residents since the spring floods of 1904 and 1905 had inundated residential and commercial areas stretching from the river to the bluffs nearly a mile to the west. No other politician in the campaign said so frequently or so bluntly, "Let's protect the West Side and not talk about it for a couple of years." Encroachment of the river channel by factory owners, carelessly at best and unlawfully at worst, was only the most visible sign of the power of the special interests, according to Ellis. "The rich men have stolen property on both sides of the river," he argued, making the channel too narrow, so that flooding could occur any time. "The men who have stolen this land should give it back to the city."[12]

Similarly, Ellis appealed to a variety of ethnic workers and neighborhoods in his promise to promote equal enforcement of the liquor laws. One hot topic focused on illegal Sunday drinking. Although some taverns looked to be closed, their front entrances tightly shuttered, patrons who knew the score could slip in through the alley door or back entrance and imbibe until some overly zealous novice on the police force tried to enforce the law. But while the poor working-man had to resort to backdoor tactics to get a drink on Sunday, the Peninsular

Club and other private clubs were legally open and serving alcohol to members. Club members saw the distinction as a difference between public and private drinking, but Ellis assailed this attitude by calling for "high-toned hotels and low-grade grog shops" to share in the spirit of the law, not merely the letter.[13]

In terms of governmental reform, Ellis pledged a program true to the progressive goals of the period: civil service examinations for office holders and citywide adoption of initiative, recall, and referendum. To balance out the older pattern of appointments "made up from the aristocratic classes and worn-out politicians who could not be elected to office by the people," Ellis guaranteed the appointment of working men. Wage earners would be given a share in running the city, he promised. After he won the election, Ellis was as good as his word. "There is no demand for bosses who profess to know more about the needs of a municipality than does the combined intelligence of its citizens," the new mayor declared in his inaugural address.

In order to stand for mayor, Ellis first had to defeat his Republican opponents in a primary election. A recently enacted charter revision had eliminated party caucuses, and for the first time, registered voters selected candidates for city offices directly in a run-off primary.[14] On the weekend before the primary, 120 newsboys, ten in each ward, distributed fliers that included Ellis's platform along with his photograph. By the end of that Saturday, an estimated 20,000 copies had been spread around town.[15] This new technique of campaigning down on the hustings to attract primary votes not only proved Ellis's ability as a campaigner, but also showed how much support this so-called "false friend" of the workingman could muster. The *Civic News* hoped the people would repudiate Ellis and nominate a "responsible" Republican standard bearer, but Ellis showed his command of the new electoral system and emerged victorious as the Republican candidate for mayor.

The Opposition

Running against Ellis were two candidates, incumbent mayor Edwin F. Sweet and furniture manufacturer Charles R. Sligh. Sweet had been elected mayor in 1904 in response to the water scandal, more because he had not been implicated than for any strong personal following. He had come to Grand Rapids as a youth, read law, and gained admission to the Michigan Bar. He married well, taking as his bride a daughter of prominent businessman Edward P. Fuller, who had moved with his family to Grand Rapids in 1868 and engaged in banking and real estate development. Sweet's later record of public service included a term as a representative to the 62nd U.S. Congress in 1911-12, and as a city commissioner in 1926. He was named Assistant Secretary of Commerce under Herbert Hoover.[16]

As a candidate in 1906, Sweet was an advocate of civic reform, running on a nonpartisan ticket. He declared that voters should choose the best man and that partisan allegiances only perpetuated corruption, "deals," and special interests.

Sweet had significant support, but it was centered on the East Side and not in sufficient numbers to do Ellis any harm.

Charles R. Sligh ran on the Democratic Party ticket, also espousing a range of social and municipal reforms. The son of Scottish immigrants, Sligh had come to Grand Rapids as a young man and worked his way up the corporate ladder to become a principal sales agent for the Berkey & Gay Furniture Company. He went on to organize the Sligh Company in 1880, which became the largest producer of bedroom furniture in the nation. In addition to his factory, Sligh owned more than a billion board feet of raw timber in forest reserves in Oregon and Washington. His second marriage was to the daughter of Isaac M. Clark, whose success with his brother Melvin in the wholesale grocery business enabled Sligh and his father-in-law to form the Clark Iron Company, with assets exceeding $2 million worth of iron deposits in Minnesota's Mesabi Range.[17]

In addition to diverse economic holdings, Sligh exercised significant political influence dating from before the turn of the century. He had served as president of the Grand Rapids Furniture Manufacturers Association and the Grand Rapids Board of Trade and was the director of several major banks. In 1896 he joined the fusion ticket of Democrats, Silver Republicans, and Populists to run for governor. Defeated by Hazen S. Pingree, he nevertheless remained active and prominent in state political affairs, accepting appointment by Governor Chase S. Osborn in 1912 to serve on the committee that helped author one of the nation's first worker compensation laws. Sligh would edge very close to Ellis's lead in the mayoral election of 1908, but in 1906 he had to share a distant second place with Edwin F. Sweet.[18]

The perception of Sweet and Sligh as members of the ruling elite did not endear them to great numbers of wage earners, although their stance on liquor control did help among some of the Dutch Calvinist voters. They also lacked the common touch and connections wielded by Ellis. Neither candidate had extensive fraternal connections beyond the Peninsular Club and the Kent Country Club.[19] Nor did they venture beyond staged lunchtime rallies to register new voters or hand out literature as Ellis did. Their patrician campaign style, moral-reform platforms, and class affiliation did little to generate enthusiasm among the working-class electorate.

Victory

The emphasis on personality, political connections, and the issue of liquor control placed Ellis far ahead of his opponents on election day. He carried every ward west of the river and on the East Side prevailed in the wards north and south of the hilltop and business districts. Ethnic and class support fell clearly into precinct lines, as lower-income wage earners and predominantly Polish neighborhoods supported Ellis. The ethnically mixed Fifth Ward, a neighborhood of poorer laborers, mostly native-born Americans along with Canadian and British immigrants, swung heavily for Ellis, as did the East Side's Brickyard Poles.

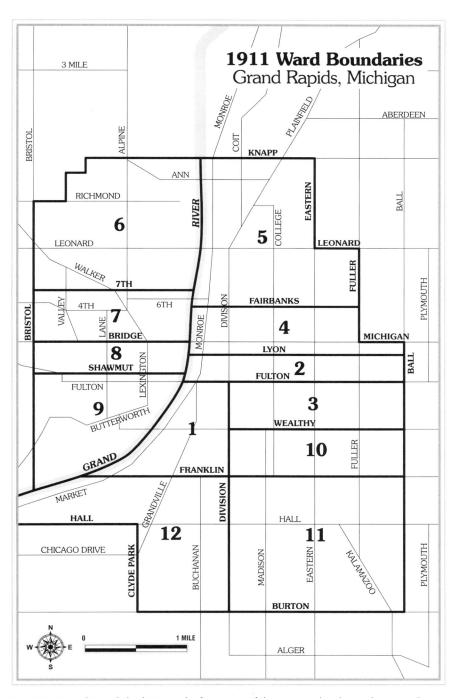

In 1911, Grand Rapids had 12 wards, four west of the river and eight on the eastside, each electing aldermen to serve on the City Council.

The only serious contest in a working-class or ethnic precinct came in the First Ward's fourth precinct, where a mix of Dutch Reformed and German Catholic votes gave Ellis a three-vote victory over Charles Sligh.[20]

Edwin Sweet and Charles Sligh had fairly respectable showings in some wards, but each pulled only half the total votes that Ellis did. Ironically, Sweet carried the Third Ward, Ellis's home territory, which was occupied primarily by professionals and industrialists. He split with Charles Sligh in the prosperous Second and Tenth wards, leaving Ellis to carry the remaining majority of votes. Support for Sweet and Sligh in the Second, Third, and Tenth wards was concentrated along the outer edge of the city, where the second-generation Dutch, respectable small businessmen, and middle-class salaried workers had begun to develop new residential neighborhoods.[21]

The Polish bloc, estimated at a total of 1,500 to 2,000 votes, was central to Ellis's victory, and it made great political sense for him to build up the Polish vote as part of his West Side coalition. The two personal secretaries who remained by his side throughout his political life, Stanley Jackowski and, later, Roman Glocheski, were from St. Adalbert's parish, a fact that could hardly go unnoticed by Polish voters. Nor could Ellis's stand for more licensing and broader distribution of saloons have hurt him in the Polish precincts, in light of the fact that Poles owned nearly 15 percent of the saloons then operating in Grand Rapids. Barroom ownership as an easy way to get ahead, providing self-employment and prestige while requiring minimal capital and few technical skills. Many an aspiring saloonkeeper needed political clout to get a liquor license, and George Ellis was their man.[22]

Instrumental to Ellis's success was his membership in a wide range of working-class fraternal organizations throughout the city. This extensive network of contacts ran the gamut from the upper stratum of the Masons to the Knights of Pythias and wound its way to the Loyal Order of Moose, the Benevolent and Protective Order of Elks, Woodmen of the World, and even to the women's Order of the Eastern Star. In later campaigns, civic reformers would bemoan Ellis's alliances with so many "fraternal assemblies" and berate him soundly for trying to "work the fraternal racket."[23]

Ellis's club connections alone could not have won over such a large percentage of the popular vote. Part of the reason for his victory rested in his campaign techniques and skill as a stump speaker. One campaign event in particular demonstrated his ability to turn a personal slight into a political triumph. At a well-attended lunchtime rally at the Bissell Carpet Sweeper Company, the manager did not provide Ellis with either a speaking platform or an introduction as he had for the "respectable" candidates. Grabbing a packing crate, Ellis stood up and said, "You know me – not them – they need an introduction." He launched into his campaign speech and received an enthusiastic response.[24]

Ellis also benefited from the recent "mass-meeting craze" in which hundreds of men (women could not yet vote) came to hear the mayoral candidates. He appeared two or three times in the course of the campaign at all the major West Side neighborhood meeting halls. Greater exposure to the voters was an out-growth of the direct primary, which stimulated voter curiosity even as it required more work for the political campaigners. The normally staid *Herald* reported a wave of voter registrations, generally among men previously ignored, and charged that the new voters were recruited while they lounged in barrooms, rooming houses, and other locales not generally associated with political activity.[25] Apparently the approach bore fruit. The turnout in 1906 was the largest recorded to that date in the city's history.

Beginning with his success in 1906, George Ellis built a coalition of working- and middle-class voters that enabled him to hold on to the mayor's office through five successive elections over ten years (at the time Grand Rapids mayors and aldermen served two-year terms). Over time, his skills as a cam-paigner, conciliator, and administrator broadened his appeal, closing the many deep-seated ethnic and religious differences among residents at election time. Ellis's victories did not mean that a solid working-class consciousness had swept traditional rivalries aside and replaced them with a unified political response. Instead it was his deft leadership and better organization, combined with the manufacturers' political weakness, that limited the industrialists and bankers to ward-level influence. Deacon Ellis could — and did — represent the average wage earner better than the factory owners could ever have done.

The mayoral election of 1906 was a visible expression of working-class con-servatism and the ambiguities of Progressive Era reform. The main issues in the campaign had been protection of private property coupled with the desire for an honest and open city administration. Ellis promised the protection of residential property from flooding caused by industrial overdevelopment along the riverbanks and the safeguarding of property values by reassessing and re-aligning tax burdens. His pledge of an honest and open administration brought the appointment of industrial workers to service boards and longer office hours for the mayor. Anything beyond this was rejected. Lukewarm efforts by Ellis in 1906 and afterwards to promote progressive reforms such as initiative, recall, and referendum failed, and were repudiated by the same voters who had put him in office. The majority of wage-earning men in Grand Rapids did not want drastic changes in the structure of their city government.

It was the hilltop manufacturers and bankers who most desired deep-seated changes in the government, but they were unable to muster support beyond the ward level. Part of their problem was the lack of a spokesman with Ellis's per-sonal appeal and political abilities. Without an articulate and sympathetic figure to carry their message effectively to a citywide audience, the industrialists would never find enough support to capture City Hall.

City Leaders

George "Deacon" Ellis served as mayor during the furniture strike. His sympathy for the strikers led the furniture men to organize a successful campaign to change the city charter. (GRPL, 54-26-11)

William D. McFarlane was the chief organizer and strike leader for the United Brotherhood of Carpenters and Joiners of America. (GRPL, Grand Rapids News, May 12, 1911)

The Rev. Alfred Wishart of Fountain Street Baptist Church was a strong proponent of the Social Gospel movement, which held that owners should be concerned about the working conditions and compensation offered their workers, and that workers, in turn, should not withhold their labor. (GRPL, 54-37-47)

Harry Widdicomb was one of the most outspoken factory owners, angering strikers when he imported strike breakers to keep his John Widdicomb Company operating. (GRPL, 185-3- 41)

Robert W. Irwin, head of the Royal Furniture Company, took a more moderate stance, supporting shorter hours and improved compensation. (GRPL, 84-22-3)

City attorney W. Millard Palmer supported the proposed city charter change creating the commission-manager form of government. (GRPL, 54-32-32)

Prominent banker Clay Hollister supported the Citizens League's efforts to change the Grand Rapids city charter. (GRPL, 54-28-50)

Former mayor George R. Perry attempted a comeback following the strike, running against Mayor George Ellis. (GRPL, 54-32-48)

William Oltman served on the city charter commission and was later elected mayor in 1922. (GRPL, 54-32-25)

George P. Tilma, former city treasurer, narrowly defeated five-term mayor George Ellis in 1916 to take the city's highest elective office. (GRPL, 54-36-12)

The Reverend Wishart

During the summer of 1906, members of the Fountain Street Baptist Church sought a replacement for their retiring minister, J.H. Randall, to lead one of the city's most prestigious congregations.[26] William Gay, head of the Berkey & Gay Furniture Company and founder of the Grand Rapids Furniture Manufacturers Association, led the four-man search team. Joining him were three other respected businessmen: Charles Hamilton, sales manager for Berkey & Gay; Frank Leonard, president of H. Leonard and Sons, importer of "fancy crockery, crystal and household furnishing"; and James Hawkins, city treasurer.[27]

The reputable men of the Fountain Street Church knew what sort of leader their congregation required. They were not blind to the changes taking place around them: the rise of furniture manufacturing to the apogee of the city's economy, the change in the city's ethnic and religious structure, and the unflagging and essential support from the West Side Polish Catholic population that George Ellis had drawn. In searching for a man to lead the church and maintain its continued prominence, they sought a pastor attuned to the city's social conditions as well as to the variety of religious experiences flooding America.

Gay and his committee found their man in Alfred Wesley Wishart, a graduate of the John D. Rockefeller-endowed University of Chicago Divinity School. Ordained in 1895, Wishart had worked since then as a minister at the Baptist Central Church of Trenton, New Jersey. There he established a regional reputation, bringing the religious and secular spheres closer together by creating the first of several "civic revivals" and serving a three-year stint as editor of one of the city's daily papers. Putting morality into practice, he founded the Anti-Bribery Society of Mercer County, New Jersey.

Wishart's concern for the working class gained national recognition when, in the wake of the 1902 silk workers strike in nearby Paterson, New Jersey, he defended English labor organizer William MacQueen against charges of inciting riots. Wishart prepared an elaborate 38-page brief in defense of MacQueen, whose case had become an international *cause célébre,* bringing in such notables to his defense as *Outlook* editor Lyman Abbott and author and social critic H.G. Wells. In the fall of 1906, the congregation of Fountain Street Baptist Church voted to accept the recommendation of their search committee and bring Wishart to its pulpit.

Alfred Wishart thought of himself as a disciple of the Social Gospel, a movement within mainstream American churches that sought to use religious doctrine as a basis for the concrete reform of economic injustice and political corruption, and for the general improvement of the quality of life. Breaking with the older notion that religious leaders should concern themselves with guiding souls to rewards in otherworldly matters, Social Gospel advocates believed firmly in the need for the church to become involved in the issues of secular society.[28] Their message echoed through America's major cities – not only New York and Chicago, but dozens of lesser industrial centers such as Paterson, Trenton, Detroit, Cleveland, Milwaukee, and Grand Rapids.

Wishart's Gospel

By training and by temperament, Wishart belonged to the conservative school of the Social Gospel, whose members tended to have been born after the Civil War and educated in the Midwest. They were generally less liberal than Easterners in their attitudes towards immigrants, unions, and government regulation of business.[29] They emphasized the new problems of city life, especially the harsh living and working conditions created by industrialization and the growing immigrant labor force.[30] Wishart's sermons repeatedly denounced critics of the Social Gospel who wished a return to the days when preachers asked men to care only for the state of their own souls, rather than the conditions confronting their fellow man. But while he championed the role of religion in providing a strong moral basis for reform in the new urban industrial environment, he felt that the initiative to correct conditions belonged to local business and religious leaders.

The Grand Rapids business community approved of Wishart's attitudes towards the current problems of the day. They recognized the need to improve urban living conditions and expressed a paternal interest in their employees' welfare while sharing his strongly held anti-Catholic, anti-union sentiments. They also agreed with his support of new industrial management techniques that stressed concentration of power into the hands of professional managers and efficiency experts. Wishart's criticisms of the Catholic Church and labor unions stemmed from a concern that membership in these groups diverted worker loyalties to larger "outside" institutions, sapping community cohesion. Wishart denied the importance of class identity for the same reason. Community fragmentation impaired productivity and generated discord, both ultimately harming the prospects for a democratic society. Wishart asserted that the new economic conditions and burgeoning urban populations must be confronted and controlled, and it was his advocacy of control that placed him at the heart of conservative reform in the Progressive Era.[31]

Wishart presented his new congregation with a set of points listing issues for reform and how to achieve them. The question was not if the church had a social mission, but what that mission was. The greatest challenge was inducing "good citizenship" and fostering involvement in civic affairs to bring private morality from the church into daily life. "It is the bad citizenship of otherwise good men," asserted Wishart, "that delays the suppression of many civic evils and hinders the progress of society."

Reform involved solving the problems of the new economic order on a "scientific" basis, Wishart contended, for "as a consequence of scientific inquiry, the new view of charity insists that there are social as well as individual causes of poverty, sickness and crime." It was chiefly through the cooperation of the public and private spheres, his reasoning went, that lasting reform could occur. In this worldview, local government assumed paramount importance. The bases for tenement reform, factory safety, and pure food all rested on understanding the relationship "between corrupt or inefficient government and the social welfare."

While believing that "it is the social mission of the church to encourage the people to do more and more for themselves," Wishart also urged greater local government involvement. He believed that "by public taxation needed social enterprises can be conducted on a much broader scale and far more effectively than by the church." The recent past, he said, has shown a tendency in modern democracy "toward a government paternal or fraternal, at any rate a government that is daily extending its care over the young, the poor, the sick, the defective and delinquents." Such developments were good, he maintained, contrary to the stand taken by those "blinded by prejudice and medieval dogmas."[32]

One of the greatest challenges confronting the church in its social mission was bridging the gap between the classes. Wishart believed that the church possessed the means of bringing all classes together. "No institution on earth has such inherent, democratic possibilities, or possesses such a brotherly philosophy of life as the Christian Church." The rich and the poor, employer and wage earner, could come together under the banner of God, but achieving progress towards this secular millennium would be difficult, especially in light of the nation's growing labor movement.

Champion of the Elite

Wishart spoke the employers' language. The rise of the American Federation of Labor offended many industrialists; the challenge by "Big Bill" Haywood and the Industrial Workers of the World frightened them. Both the AFL and IWW had been active in New Jersey at the time of Wishart's tenure there and made an appearance during the silk workers strike. Little wonder then that he believed, "The working class are feverish, restless, pushing forward under strange standards, inspired by ideals and led by men outside the church to which many of them are indifferent or hostile."[33]

From his Grand Rapids pulpit, Wishart assured the influential members of Fountain Street Church that the path they had adopted in dealing with economic and political issues was morally correct. "Society," he told the congregation, "is not wrong in looking to its industrial leaders" for the solution of industrial problems. He also recognized the growing contest between employer and wage earner for power in this new arena. "Modern democracy tends inevitably toward an increase in the economic wants of the masses and their desire for a larger share in the control of industrial, social and political conditions." The furniture manufacturers, he said, had taken steps in the right direction by cooperating with each other to promote stability. The Furniture Manufacturers Association and the Employers Association properly worked to "eliminate waste in production and distribution, to lessen the evils of competition," and to help one and all secure the blessings of prosperity.

What the Federal Trade Commission would come to view as an illegal conspiracy to fix prices in the furniture trust Wishart saw as a laudable effort "to maintain just prices" and avoid the "dishonorable practice" of price cutting. When Wishart spoke of cooperation to promote social harmony, he meant cooperation among employers "to work unselfishly together...through organized effort." The pursuit of stability and profit went hand in glove, he said, since economic efficiency "is absolutely essential to the well being of individuals and the best interest of society. Hence every manufacturer should be a special student of all those plans classed under the title of 'scientific management.'"

The nation's leading advocate of scientific management was Frederick Winslow Taylor, who advocated "rationalizing" the workplace through such devices as time-motion studies. He and his fellow efficiency experts argued that scientific management was not only a "device to secure increased production," but was "a method in industry which is bound to be followed by industrial and social results of vast importance...." Wishart embraced the notion that scientific management, not the work of unionization, brought progress, declaring, "Organized labor has very little...to do with the general advance of human beings in this country." Arguing that only a "limited number of [unionized] workers" had seen any improvement in wages and working conditions, he concluded that organized labor was "not the cause for the economic advance of the American people."

Clearly the efforts of owners and management were in conflict with the union ideal of collective action among workers. "Jesus taught the stewardship of wealth," maintained the Fountain Street pastor, "that all men have obligations." Some men were meant to lead and others to follow, some to disburse the fruits of stewardship and others to benefit. Collective action by workers was at best negligible, at worst disruptive of the process by which wealth was created and distributed. Labor unions could only produce disruption that "breeds poverty."

In Wishart's view, economic progress was tied directly to the new industrial system, and this new system demanded the subordination of labor. Any sort of collective action by workers threatened the emerging order. Wishart's praises for scientific management were not merely attempts to laud the most recent developments in managerial theory. He understood clearly that Taylorism was a tool to stop unionization before it started, especially in older productive processes, such as furniture manufacturing, that were making the shift towards greater dependence on machines and mass production.[34]

Alfred Wishart acted on his beliefs. From the time of his arrival in 1906 until his death in 1933, he served the business community in a capacity unmatched by any other clergyman in Grand Rapids. He was especially involved in the Grand Rapids Board of Trade, precursor to the Chamber of Commerce, where his work carried him far beyond the traditional breakfast prayers or service on the speakers board assumed by many ministers. Chairing the trade board's Committee on Social Affairs, he led the movement for playground and park expansion and, after 1917, the drive to Americanize immigrants. Motivated to refute charges in the daily papers that the Board of Trade conspired to oust the Brunswick-Balke Company because it was represented by outside ownership and managers, he inaugurated an investigation to prove that the firm relocated for selfish reasons, selling out to the highest municipal bidder. Wishart also played a key role on the Municipal Committee's search for administrative fraud in city government in 1914-15. This work led to the establishment of a new charter commission and eventually the council-manager form of city government.[35]

With time, Wishart's reputation spread beyond the city. The Ramona Theater in Grand Rapids filled to capacity on Sunday afternoons as nearly 2,000 people turned out to hear his sermons on current social topics. These sermons and other comments appeared in the regionally important business journal, *Michigan Investor,* suggesting that his brand of the Social Gospel appealed to many outside the Grand Rapids Board of Trade. Finally, his national impact became apparent when Clarence Darrow traveled to Grand Rapids in 1928 to debate him on "The Meaning of Life." At his death in 1933, Wishart received tribute from Harry Emerson Fosdick, nationally acknowledged leader of the Social Gospel movement in America, who called Wishart "a devoted Christian, a great preacher, a fearless liberal, and intelligent and forward looking citizen."[36]

A City Divided

The election of George Ellis and the arrival of Alfred Wishart represented two dramatically different approaches to reform. Divided by the ends they sought to achieve and the means by which to achieve them, these opposing views helped to polarize Grand Rapids in the years after 1906. For the group centered on George Ellis and the Republican Party, the agenda was a program of social justice in which the wage-earning population might have a more direct say in the operation of city government. They believed the established political machinery was good enough to redress the issues of unequal property assessment and riverfront development.[37]

With his support built upon a coalition of middle- and working-class neighborhoods, both Catholic and Protestant, Ellis came to rely upon the decisive impact of bloc voting from the West Side. His attacks on the "selfish rich" and his efforts to steer a moderate middle ground through the moral issues of saloon control and Sunday theater closings drew increasing wrath from the city's business leaders and self-styled reformers. His close ties to the immigrant Catholic community brought charges of political bossism and further exacerbated his differences with the "respectable" citizens of Grand Rapids.

During the decade Ellis spent in the mayor's seat, he moved towards reform measures that included housing codes, eight-hour days for city employees, and wider participation by working-class men on municipal boards. However, the conservative nature of his coalition, made up of home-owning wage earners, balked at any deep-seated change in the structure of city government, and his constituency defeated a 1912 charter proposal, which he endorsed, that called for publicly owned utilities among other reforms.

Although Alfred Wishart spoke officially for the Fountain Street Baptist Church, his comments addressed the concerns of progressive men everywhere on the city's east side. His attitudes towards unions, Catholicism, and industrial management served as the locus for a growing party of discontent with the new economic and political world of the industrial city. But the reform coalition he represented lacked the political leadership and cohesion of Ellis and the Republican Party. For one thing, Wishart's emphasis on secular matters drove a wedge between his Baptist congregation and the Calvinist communities that were trying desperately to keep out of "worldly matters," creating friction between two Protestant groups who might otherwise have found common cultural ground.

Without an effective political organization, the hilltop denizens skittered about, flailing at Ellis's presumed moral corruption, occasionally pulling in support from the middle-class neighborhoods to the south by pressing concrete issues such as saloon licensing and Sunday theater closings. But their candidates never quite grasped the importance of widespread political support at the local ward level or engaged in the sort of face-to-face politicking that Ellis did so well.

More important, they insisted that moral reform could come about only through legally binding ordinances — saloon licenses must be regulated by the exercise of the law; limits on the number of saloons must be drawn up and districts designated and patrolled. At the same time that it increased suspicion among ordinary workingmen, this hard-nosed position stood in contrast to Ellis's attitude of compromise in the city council, where give and take among aldermen might best secure the needs of their wards.

After 1906, the two camps competed for control of the city government, sharing the belief that the older mercantile leaders had lost touch with the issues that most affected the city and were about to pass from the scene. Each faction pressed for a variety of reforms, and although Ellis and his followers prevailed initially, in the end power shifted into the hands of Wishart, the industrialists, and their fellow structural reformers. Interestingly, it was the furniture strike of 1911, the high point of labor activism in Grand Rapids up to that time, that proved to many wavering middle-class residents that the industrial and commercial leaders were right, that city government as it was structured could not be trusted to act impartially in times of industrial crisis. Ellis's thoroughgoing support for the furniture workers strike that debilitated the city throughout the summer of 1911 made him anathema, and if his power could not be weakened under the established political system, then the system must be changed.

The same decade in which Wishart and Ellis clashed over the nature of reform saw an increasing rate of home ownership in the city coupled with a sharp decline in the number of workers employed by the furniture industry. The proportion of furniture workers fell from nearly 34 percent of the total workforce in

1910 to less than 25 percent by 1920.[38] As fewer workers shared common employment experiences, the principal bridge among wage earners became not class-consciousness as workers, but property-consciousness as homeowners. This broad-based commitment to the security of private property would eventually provide the votes necessary for Grand Rapids' hilltop business and financial leaders to change the direction of city government and take over the reins of political power.

Endnotes

1. Several historians have commented on the emerging political power of wealthy industrialists in the late 19th and early 20th centuries in American cities. See for example: Samuel P. Hays, "The Changing Political Structure of the City in Industrial America," *Journal of Urban History* 1 (November, 1974), pp. 6-38; Herbert Gutman, "Class, Status and Community Power in Nineteenth Century Industrial Cities: Paterson, New Jersey: A Case Study" in *Work, Culture and Society in Industrializing America* (New York: Random House, 1976), pp. 234-59; Robert Wiebe, *The Search for Order.*

2. Gordon Olson, *A Grand Rapids Sampler,* (Grand Rapids: Grand Rapids Historical Commission, 1992), p. 123; Z. Z. Lydens, *The Story of Grand Rapids* (Grand Rapids: Kregel Publications), pp. 57-65, 92, 406.

3. For more on the League's activities, see *Civic News* reports on the City Council meetings, May through June 1906, plus records of the City Council. For a comparison of other efforts at municipal reform and their limitations, see: Raymond R. Fragnoli, "Progressive Coalition and Municipal Reform: Charter Revision in Detroit 1912-1918," *Detroit in Perspective: A Journal of Regional History* 4 (Spring, 1980), pp. 118-42; Jack D. Elenbaas, "The Boss of the Better Class: Henry Leland and the Detroit Citizens League, 1912-1924," *Michigan History* 58 (Spring, 1974), pp. 131-45; Thomas A. Scott, "The Diffusion of Urban Governmental Forms as a Case Study of Social Learning," *Journal of Politics* 30 (1968), pp. 1091-1108; Bradley R. Rice, *Progressive Cities: The Commission Government Movement in America 1901-1920* (Austin: University of Texas Press, 1977).

4. Arthur C. Milispaugh, *Party Organization and Machinery in Michigan Since 1890* (Baltimore: Johns Hpkins University Press, 1917); Stephen B. and Vera H. Sarasohn, *Political Parties in Michigan* (Detroit: Wayne State University Press, 1957), pp. 8-19.

5. Anthony R. Travis, "Mayor George Ellis: Grand Rapids Political Boss and Progressive Reformer," *Michigan History* 58 (Spring, 1974), pp. 101-30; Lynn G. Mapes, "Flamboyant Mayor George Ellis," *Grand Rapids Magazine* (January, 1976) p. 24.

6. *Civic News,* December 16, 1905, pp. 1-3; "Bucket Shop Department Store," pamphlet published by the Good Government League of Grand Rapids (n.d.); Cedric Cowing, *Populists, Plungers and Progressives: A Social History of Stock and Commodity Speculation* (Princeton: Princeton University Press, 1969).

7. *Civic News,* December 1, 1906; *National Cyclopedia of Biography.*

8. *Civic News,* March 3, 1906, p. 1. March 30, 1906, p. 1, April 1, 1906, p. 1. See also the *Michigan Tradesman* for March 23, 1910. Similar sentiments were voiced by Edwin Sweet's supporters in the *Herald,* March 16, 1906.

9. *Civic News,* May 12, 1906, p. 1; *Herald,* May 8, 1906, p. 5.

10. *Herald,* April 20, 1906, p. 1.

11. Ibid. p. 6.

12. *Herald,* April 1, 1906, p. 2.

13. Ibid. March 9, 1906, p. 6.
14. City Charter of the City of Grand Rapids, 1905.
15. *Herald,* March 11, 1906, p. 6.
16. *National Cyclopedia of Biography.*
17. Ibid.
18. Ibid.
19. *Dau's Blue Book and Social Reporter for Grand Rapids* (Chicago: Dau's Blue Book Inc., 1906).
20. *Herald,* April 7, 1906, pp. 1-2. Election results of April 7, 1906, in *Herald, Evening Press* and *Evening News.* The newspapers remain the only sources of final results since much original material was destroyed when Grand Rapids' old City Hall was torn down in 1967.
21. Ibid.
22. Ibid.; Mapes, "Flamboyant Mayor George Ellis," p. 24; Anthony R. Travis, "Mayor George Ellis: Grand Rapids Political Boss and Progressive Reformer," pp. 101-30; see also Edward Pinkowski, "The Great Influx of Polish Immigrants and the Industries They Entered" in Frank Mocha, ed., *Poles in America: Bicentennial Essays* (Stevens Point: Worzalla Publishing Co., 1978), pp. 303-70. Michigan had the fifth largest Polish population in the United States in 1910.
23. "Some Racy Reading," Good Government League of Grand Rapids (1914), p. 2.
24. *Herald,* March 30, 1906, p. 5.
25. Mapes, "Flamboyant Mayor," p. 24.
26. Register of members and pew rentals for 1906 show many hilltop addresses and members of the new industrial elite, such as William Gay and Robert Irwin.
27. *Herald,* May 7, 1906.
28. Henry L. May, *Protestant Churches and Industrial America* (New York: Harper & Brothers, 1949); Ronald C. White and C. Howard Hopkins, *The Social Gospel: Religion and Reform in Changing America* (Philadelphia: Temple University Press, 1976).
29. Ferenc Szaz, "Protestantism and the Search for Stability: Liberal and Conservative Quests for a Christian America, 1875-1925" in Jerry Israel, ed., *Building the Organizational Society* (New York: Free Press, 1970); William R. Hutchinson, "Cultural Strain and Protestant Liberalism," *American Historical Review* 76 (April, 1971), pp. 386-411; Ralph E. Luker, "The Social Gospel and the Failure of Radical Reform, 1877-1898," *Church History* 46 (March, 1977), pp. 80-99.
30. For more on immigrants and reform, see Gerd Korman, *Industrialization, Immigrants and Americanizers: The View from Milwaukee, 1866-1921* (Madison: State Historical Society of Wisconsin, 1967); Joseph R. Gusfield, *Symbolic Crusade: Status Politics and the American Temperance Movement* (Urbana: University of Illinois Press, 1966); John Higham, *Strangers in the Land* (New York: Atheneum, 1972).
31. Alfred W. Wishart, "Sermon Preached January 13, 1907" (n.p., n.d.), pp. 1-21.
32. Wishart, "The Social Mission of the Church" (American Baptist Social Service Commission of the Northern Baptist Convention, 1909), pp. 15, 17, 40-41.
33. Ibid. p. 47.
34. Wishart, "Industrial Democracy: An Address Delivered Before the National Furniture Manufacturers Association in Grand Rapids, December 1, 1915," pp. 11, 13, 14.
35. Based on *Minutes* of the Board of Directors, Board of Trade of Grand Rapids, an analysis of committee assignments, members and reports 1908-1933.
36. *Evening Press,* April 26, 1933, p. 1.
37. Melvin Holli, *Reform in Detroit* (New York: Oxford University Press, 1967); for a review of the literature see Michael Frisch, "Oyez, Oyez, Oyez: The Recurring Case of Plunkett v. Steffens," *Journal of Urban History* 7 (February, 1981), pp. 205-18.
38. Figures based on Michigan Department of Labor, *Reports,* for 1906-1918, and the Fourteenth Federal Census.

Chapter 4

Collective Bargaining and the Right to Strike:
The Matter of Control

The fracture lines of class, neighborhood, religion, and ethnicity widened into chasms during the 1911 strike by the city's furniture workers. Although the immediate concerns were wages, hours, and working conditions, the core issue was control over the workplace. Embedded in the controversy was a concern among the factory owners that loss of control through union organization and representation would mean the loss of power in the political arena, particularly over issues of zoning and taxation. Should the wage earners through collective bargaining successfully challenge their economic influence, the industrialists and financiers feared the economic system they had built would begin to unravel.

Worker Dissatisfaction

Worker unrest in the furniture industry had been growing for some time. As far back as November 1909, a three-man committee, representing 45 skilled cabinetmakers out of a workforce of more than 300, asked management at the Oriel plant for a cost-of-living increase. The request for wages more in line with inflation was not unreasonable. The Grand Rapids newspapers of the time all noted the increased cost of food, and one of the city's aldermen even suggested a boycott among consumers to drive down food prices. Even the popular fifteen-cent dinner served in most working-class diners had disappeared. Instead of recognizing the legitimacy of the workers' concerns, the Oriel plant owner in January 1910 dismissed the three men as "agitators."[1]

In October 1910 employee dissatisfaction with working conditions came to a head when 4,000 workers across the city organized informally and voted to request an adjustment of the current piece-rate system along with increased wages and shorter hours. The piece-rate structure, in which workers were paid a set figure for each piece they finished – whether a chair leg, dresser drawer, or piece of ornamentation — regardless of how long it took, was a particular sticking point. Workers wanted a set pay rate per hour of work. Exercising their collective clout through a brief walkout in December 1910 brought the workers promises from one factory owner that "beyond question, after the first of January [1911], what they requested would be granted."[2]

When the promised changes did not occur, employees from around the city petitioned members of the Furniture Manufacturers Association to conduct collective bargaining sessions. Their goal was to establish a binding agreement for uniform policies in all the factories regarding wages, hours, and working conditions. The fact of the matter was that the manufacturers, through their Employers Association, already did this, but without any regard to the wishes of the workers. That wage earners wanted a say in the terms of their employment was an unthinkable precedent that owners sought to avoid at all costs. It did not matter that, with the exception of a relatively small number of skilled craftsmen, workers' representatives had not raised the specific issue of union representation. For the manufacturers it was, at this point, still a matter of keeping any potential conflict local, private, and "all in the family."

Public awareness of the furniture workers' grievances came in March 1911, with front-page coverage in the city newspapers detailing the workers' requests and the FMA's response. Worker representatives argued that given the large number of workers involved — "all cabinet makers, machine hands, packers, trimmers...affiliated with the carpenters and joiners" — collective bargaining would be the best way to solve the widespread problems. The manufacturers immediately refused to accept the proposition that workers had the right to organize and have their demands met through collective bargaining. Reiterating their desire to deal with individual workingmen, FMA members circulated a letter among all 6,000 industry workers stating that the traditional policy of each firm has always been to recognize "the liberty of every man, union or nonunion, without discrimination, to sell his labor freely, independently and at the best price obtainable."[3]

The Grand Rapids Employers Association sent its secretary Francis Campau to act as spokesman to the public. Campau, the grandson of Grand Rapids founder Louis Campau's brother Antoine, assailed the workers' requests, claiming that employees received first-rate treatment at the hands of the employers, who had voluntarily raised wages over the past year. Reduced hours — specifically the nine-hour day — were "virtually a fact" ever since Saturday had become a half-holiday. There were no grounds for complaint, according to Campau, only an unwarranted interference by wage earners into the affairs of private business.[4]

A War of Words

The running war of words continued unabated through early March, as William McFarlane, national organizer for the United Brotherhood of Carpenters and Joiners, took to the newspapers to condemn Campau's position. McFarlane's appearance in Grand Rapids was testimony that the dispute was no longer only a local issue. The brotherhood, a national union affiliated with the American Federation of Labor, had taken an interest in working conditions in Grand Rapids, imperiling the local manufacturers' one-sided control of their isolated workers. McFarlane's key point that "organized bargaining" benefited all parties exposed the fact that the manufacturers had been working in concert while denying workers the same prerogative. His public statements in the Grand Rapids papers brought to light the fact that businesses in other cities across the country, run by people with "wide experience in the large commercial and manufacturing centers," had successfully shared some degree of workplace control without endangering their enterprises.[5]

Even as McFarlane wrote his reply to Campau, the Grand Rapids Show Case Company moved to undercut union sympathies among its employees and discourage attempts at unionization and collective bargaining by giving its skilled workers a raise of nearly two dollars per week. Precipitated by the growing labor unrest, this attempt to defuse worker demands for a 10 percent across-the-board increase was the second raise in as many months. But the divide-and-conquer tactic failed. Attempts by FMA members to separate workers from union-led collective action bore little fruit as tensions increased and local newspapers began writing of a possible strike.

The *Evening News* published a series of editorials, neutral in tone, asking both parties to avoid the disruption of a strike or lockout. One editorial, entitled "Wisdom and Folly," drew parallels between the impending local conflict and the recently failed 1910 typographers strike in Chicago. The ill feelings engendered by such a strike, said the *News,* could be avoided through collective bargaining, compromise, and the realization that all the city's residents depended upon each other. Why not submit to binding arbitration conducted through some neutral third party and strengthen the city's industrial system with a series of "collective contracts"? Citing the FMA's letter sent earlier to the furniture factory workforce, the editorial noted that "it is the meanest employer in any line of business that fixes the standard of wages in the particular industry" and argued that collective bargaining remained the "only effective safeguard against this conceded industrial evil."[6]

Sustaining its arguments on the front page with evidence from a recent state industrial report, the *Evening News* refuted Campau's claims to adequate wage levels by pointing out that the city's furniture workers, who were earning slightly more than $2.50 per day, fared worse than their counterparts in other Michigan cities. Examining the evidence, the *Evening News* found that average pay raises in Grand Rapids ran to 3.5 percent instead of the 7-14 percent claimed by the industrialists. The increase in real terms for the typical worker came to nine cents a day. The newspaper articles may have been meant to shame the furniture manufacturers to the bargaining table, but in fact only prompted rebuttal by the employers. Claiming that owners made little profit, the FMA asserted, "There is a general impression that the furniture factory employees are inadequately compensated. This may be true. But the whole industry is inadequately compensated. It offers a long history of defaulted dividends and depreciated stock."[7]

By mid-March, the war of words spilled over from the daily newspapers into the manufacturers' trade journals. Claiming to be just and fair men, the FMA members avowed complete willingness to bargain with individual employees, declaring that the workers were being misled by outside agitators with self-seeking motives. The sticking point was collective bargaining; eliminate the demand for industry-wide negotiations and there would be no trouble. Through McFarlane and other representatives, the workers responded with repeated calls for collective bargaining over the issues of hours, pay, and the piece-rate system. They claimed that only through an industry-wide agreement could fairness be guaranteed.

At the same time, collective bargaining found an unlikely champion in the Reverend F. R. Godolphin of Grace Episcopal Church. Godolphin argued from the pulpit that "trade unionism" connected modern workers with an older form of social and economic relationship: paternalism. He asserted that paternalism represented "a fair reciprocal contract between workman and employer, the employer not conferring a benefit nor the workman a favor, in short, self-respecting and mutually respecting parties freely contracting with each other." Invoking the language of industrial efficiency expert Frederick W. Taylor, the minister defended trade unions by saying they stood for "men over [the] dollar, efficiency over cheapness." As he saw it, there was "no fundamental antagonism between the church and the laboring man."[8]

As the month wore on, the *Evening News* again pushed forward with an editorial supporting the workingmen's demands and noting that their lives were inextricably interwoven with the city's greater good. "The general well being of the many," intoned the paper, "in proportion as the purchasing power of the great wage-earning classes increases or lessens, so must wax or wane the prosperity of the business classes generally."[9] The editorial maintained that higher wages would lift the prosperity of city merchants and retailers. Conversely, the failure to cut back hours or increase wages would hurt the whole of the community by depriving a significant number of residents the opportunity to participate fully as consumers in the marketplace. By pushing for low wages and unchallenged control, the furniture manufacturers dampened the whole cycle of economic growth.

This argument was given additional credence in mid-March when city newspapers announced the FMA had won a major concession from the railroads, permitting factories to pool their shipments to the West Coast and pay the same rate as cities such as Chicago, whose location and volume of shipping business had given them a decided advantage over smaller, less accessible Grand Rapids. Anyone reading stories of the settlement could see that lower rates for goods to be shipped in small quantities over a longer distance would afford a major savings to the industrialists that could be passed along to their employees. [10]

While the FMA remained silent about sharing with workers the savings gained from its railroad deal, the United Brotherhood of Carpenters and Joiners used the announcement as one more grievance in the attempt to organize laborers for a citywide strike vote. Anxious to avoid trouble, Mayor George Ellis suggested the creation of a citizens committee to arbitrate outstanding differences between the two groups, pending an investigation to determine the validity of complaints on both sides. In a letter published in the papers and also sent privately to Charles Watters, president of the District Council of Furniture Workers, the local arm of the United Brotherhood of Carpenters and Joiners, and John Mowat, secretary of the Employers Association, Ellis urged reconciliation before the conflict grew any more heated. He recommended appointment of a mayor's commission of disinterested "professional men" and clergy who might keep the city from being torn apart by impending labor difficulties. [11] Nothing came of the mayor's offer, and organizers began to prepare for a strike.

One day before the scheduled strike vote on March 25, John Mowat declined to comment. Offering only that he was home "suffering an attack of acute indigestion" and therefore could not answer any questions about the current "labor difficulties," he left city residents — and potential strikers — in the dark. Nor would Charles Watters commit any statement to print. This silence irritated the editor of the *Evening News,* who wanted some hard facts or at least some public statement of events for the paper's readers. Silence by both parties violated the public's right to know, asserted a *News* editorial, especially given that "the interests of the people of every municipality are interdependent." [12] There was plenty to write about, however, two days later when the results of the strike vote became known.

The Call to Strike

On March 25, 1911, more than 3,000 furniture wage earners converged on a West Side hall to vote on whether or not to authorize a strike. When the ballots were counted at the end of the day, an overwhelming 95 percent favored a walkout on April 1, less than a week away. Once again, the *Evening News* called for reconciliation, while Reverend Godolphin used his Sunday pulpit to endorse workers' demands and their call for a strike. Believing that popular support stood with the workers, he maintained that reconciliation could come only between equals and that a union of workers was a necessary balance to the power manufacturers held in their associations. "Unions need guidance and direction," he preached, "not crushing." Godolphin assigned the responsibility for guidance and conciliation to the church, placing the clergy at the center of the process where, given the chance, God's words and ministers could demonstrate the "practical application of righteousness to industry." [13]

The local newspaper editors agreed with Rev. Godolphin that workingmen needed to organize. Unions, they said, were a prerequisite to achieving balance and order, a way to create equilibrium between the city's two most important economic parties. Failure to allow workers to organize would disrupt the entire community and create the opportunity for unrest and even violence. The only unspoken difference between the newspapers and the minister centered on whose guiding hand should mediate differences between labor and industry.

Four days before the April strike deadline, the FMA issued its first public statement since early March. Speaking through Francis Campau, the manufacturers declined the mayor's offer of assistance, claiming that the men who voted to strike represented a small minority of the city's furniture workers. The trouble, they claimed, could be traced to a few "self-serving agitators" who worked for the carpenters union and traveled in search of gullible workers. Expressing a "profound" concern for the effects of a strike on the community, Campau assured the public "of our confidence in our ability to meet any conditions that may arise."[14] In the journal *Furniture Manufacturer and Artisan,* the FMA told a national business audience that "promoters of the agitation" had been "aided by some of the newspapers of Grand Rapids." This alliance of agitators and newspaper editors turned public opinion against the manufacturers, which, according to the journal article, would not ordinarily have been the case.[15]

On March 29, a crowd of workers numbering in the thousands attended a "monster rally." Addressed by Mayor Ellis, various members of the clergy, and John A. Lennon, a national organizer for the American Federation of Labor, the cheering throng heard how the FMA's claims of fair wages failed in the face of nationwide industrial pay. As they stood together to hear the speeches, skilled cabinetmakers and joiners who had been involved in grievances since late 1909 found common cause with the finishers and those who operated machines or performed less skilled jobs. Estimates brought the total number of strike supporters up to 4,000, a number representing the overwhelming majority of skilled workers and two-thirds the total number of furniture workers in the city.

In the wake of this popular outpouring of support for a strike, the *Evening Press* took the city's furniture manufacturers to task for their backward stance. The papers argued that the FMA's closed-mouth approach harmed the manufacturers' cause and that no business could afford to adopt a "public-be-damned" attitude. "It is hardly necessary to remind you that the world has changed," lectured the *Evening Press,* and "the attitude as WHAT IS YOUR BUSINESS AND WHAT IS OUR BUSINESS has altered. The conclusion has been reached that anything which affects OUR safety, our happiness and our pocketbooks, like a strike, is very much the public business."[16]

To most of the city's newspapers, the headlong rush to strike had to be stopped if at all possible. Trust your fellow citizens, be candid with the facts, and all things can be worked out, editorials pleaded. Yet the FMA held firm. Answering the newspapers' charges by declaring that the strike was a private issue and not a public concern, the manufacturers claimed that union recognition rather than wages stood at the heart of the matter. The Grand Rapids men argued that their operations and expectations were no different from others across the country, buttressing their claim with a letter from industrialists in Jamestown, New York. The FMA implied that the government, the newspapers, and the citizens of Grand Rapids had failed to understand that recognition of the union – or any other innovation – would only bring about unnecessary and unwelcome changes.

Presenting their case to other industrialists around the country through their trade journals, FMA members warned that "if the chief manufacturing industry in Grand Rapids can be unionized, an important step will have been taken towards unionizing all her industries."[17] In other words, according to the furniture makers, a sort of domino effect would prevail and other businesses would soon find the union wolf at their door.

On March 31, the day before the threatened strike, the *Creston News,* a self-proclaimed "independent weekly," unleashed a barrage of criticism towards FMA member behavior during the preceding four weeks. The *News* editorialized that a strike would mean that the manufacturers' private interests had defeated the public welfare. Speaking for its northeast neighborhood's predominantly blue-collar and native-born residents, the *News* argued that the furniture industry's "abnormally low" wages reflected the withholding of the workers' "fair share of the profits." What's more, a protracted strike would exaggerate the already obvious imbalance between workers and employers.

Building on the issue of equity and whether or not profit, rather than wages alone, was the basis of economic fair play, the editor spoke openly about a subject that few had treated in public: the dominant role of furniture manufacturing in the city. The "up-building of the furniture industry" had "crowded out" all other industrial activity, claimed the paper, so that "metal working trades, great mercantile houses, manufacturing plants of almost every description have failed to find a welcome in Grand Rapids because Grand Rapids has been given up to the manufacture of furniture." The FMA's response to workers was simply base ingratitude, said the *News.* How could men from the city turn their backs on the community that supported them?

Citing the familiar case of the Brunswick-Balke company being "driven" from town by the furniture men, the *Creston News* demanded to know why there were no chemical plants or automobile works in Grand Rapids, especially when such profitable and increasingly important industries were being welcomed in other cities across the state? Why should Michigan's second largest city be penalized in its efforts for urban growth? The time had come, said the *News,* "for the Board of Trade to forget initiative and referendum, the city beautiful and devote itself to the city prosperous" by assuring that all workers had a fair wage while permitting a broader industrial base to develop in the area.[18]

Seeking a Compromise

With broadsides issuing from the newspapers and trade journals, city residents were expecting fireworks on April 1. But the day came and went quietly. Although no strike materialized, the threat was no April Fools hoax. Roman Catholic Archbishop Joseph Schrembs and other prominent citizens had labored behind the scenes to avert catastrophe by trying to achieve conciliation in the form of a fact-finding committee. For the moment, strike plans were on hold.

From the outset, obvious divisions emerged. The FMA asserted that the committee should sit simply as a board of inquiry and examine the degree to which charges of low wages were true. The union advocates, meanwhile, held out hopes that the committee might become an arbitration board. Neither Bishop Schrembs nor Reverend Wishart agreed upon anything except their willingness to sit together on the board and an acknowledgement that the strike would be a terrible rupture to the community. Nor did they share a perception of what the strike's delay meant. For Schrembs, the decision to postpone action demonstrated the "conservative and thoughtful nature" of the city's workingmen. Wishart declared that such consideration had "weakened their cause."[19]

Ultimately, compromises produced agreement that the committee would serve as a forum to present all points of view. Most important, however, committee members accepted the FMA's insistence that the committee not become an arbitration board. Given the nonbinding nature of the process, so the reasoning went, there would be no ground for either withholding or falsifying information. The committee began its work on April 6 by taking workers' depositions in the lobby of the Livingston Hotel at the corner of Fulton Street and Division Avenue. The *Creston News* did not wait for the committee's findings to become public before condemning the manufacturers as oppressors of the working class, who luxuriated in their $600 automobiles and financed jaunts to Europe on the backs of laborers who brought home an average of $9 a week.

Despite the fact that no news came from the committee during the first week of April, hopes for some sort of compromise to avert a strike appeared in the city's daily papers. Even union representative McFarlane suggested that the strike could be postponed, if not canceled, once the committee's findings became public.[20] Only the *Creston News* continued to sound pessimistic notes. Announcing that the prospects for Socialist Party candidates looked very bright that year, the *News* declared that class-based issues had assumed greater importance than previously. Workers, said the paper, should be prepared for political action as well as economic struggles. The paper also asserted that truly objective, fact-finding deliberation by the committee was unlikely, given the open sympathies for wage earners by Bishop Schrembs and five other members of the seven-member committee. While that spelled good news for workers, it obviously meant that the manufacturers would have little faith in the committee's work. Although the *News* did not say so outright, the statement seemed to anticipate that the industrialists would reject any findings and thereby provoke the workers to go ahead with their strike.[21]

As Grand Rapids residents prepared to celebrate Easter, the city's daily newspapers reported that compromise seemed in the offing. Labor representative McFarlane said that no reasonable offer would be refused, while Archbishop Schrembs hoped that the manufacturers' response would "contain sufficient concessions to the men to insure its acceptance." Popular support for the workingmen and fear of social disruption had combined to create expectations that the manufacturers might bend slightly to reasonable public opinion and the compromise efforts of the city's nonpartisan fact-finding committee.

Instead of compromise, the week held only disappointment. On Tuesday, April 18, five days before Easter, city newspapers printed the FMA's response, which declared that the industrialists would not deal with workers in any form of collective bargaining. Claiming that business hardships made any other response impossible, the manufacturers shut off all further discussion.

The FMA's position shocked the community and inspired worker solidarity. The United Brotherhood of Carpenters and Joiners and the Finishers Union had gathered many new members into their ranks in the weeks since early March. Now the factory owners' stubborn resistance to change strengthened workers' resolve to walk off their jobs. Despite an earlier pledge to refrain from drastic action until the citizens committee had finished its work, at a meeting on April 18, more than 4,000 men voted to strike immediately.[22]

Out on Strike

The strike began on Wednesday, April 19, the day after the FMA response was published, when many angry workers did not report for work. The walkout quickly gained momentum as word spread and more and more workers stayed home. Soon, the majority of the city's furniture factories faced complete shutdown. Both sides had come to the point where neither workers nor employers could agree on a format for discussing problems, let alone compromise on possible solutions to their impasse. Manufacturers chafed at public discussion of what they regarded as their private business matters, while the political and popular presses saw business decisions as having an impact on the city's welfare and therefore fit subjects for public discussion.

While the furniture manufacturers scrambled to keep operating with skeleton workforces and imported strikebreakers, leaders of the United Brotherhood of Carpenters and Joiners promised striking union members 75 percent of their regular wages, assuring them they would have an income to support their households. Strengthened in their resolve, the strikers' local organizers wrote an open letter to the FMA arguing that the Grand Rapids furniture industry dominated the national trade and therefore could afford a slight increase in prices to offset any increase in wages. Manufacturers countered with an open letter asserting that the city's location was a handicap to the factories and in order to maintain any sort of competitive advantage in production and sales, wages had to be controlled. According to the manufacturers, current wages were comparable to national levels, and workers' claims that production costs in Grand Rapids were 40 percent less than anywhere else arose from ignorance of business methods and the marketplace.

Shifting their attack, strikers pointed to the control exerted by employers over the local labor market. They charged that the FMA effectively underwrote operations for the Grand Rapids Employers Association, which kept a central index-card file on every eligible worker, past and present, and used this storehouse of information to regulate wages and blacklist troublesome laborers. The FMA acknowledged that the cards did exist, but only to promote industrial efficiency. Each member firm collected its own cards, and while company officers might unofficially share the information, the Employers Association did not exist as a sinister vehicle for workplace enforcement.[23]

Although newspapers cast them as heroes in a struggle against a larger foe, the strike-idled workers raised fears in some quarters that their inactivity might prompt violence or destructive behavior or, at the very least, that they might spend too much free time in the neighborhood bars. Police commissioner William B. Weston spoke reassuringly. "The working men of Grand Rapids are not the type to cause any lawlessness or disorder and we expect none." The *Evening News* reported that from the very first steps of balloting for strike action through to the eventual walkout there had been neither "levity nor loud talking."[24]

Despite these assurances, Mayor Ellis anticipated that local taverns might be busier than usual during the daylight hours. Taking an egalitarian stand in the matter, Ellis urged reduced hours and Sunday closings for all saloons and private clubs, including the Peninsular Club. The same day, the city council passed a special resolution endorsing Ellis's "request." That evening, Ellis joined labor leaders at the Ramona Theater on nearby Reeds Lake to urge both abstinence and active picketing of the "saloons [to] keep your men from going in."[25] The 2,000 men present cheered as McFarlane promised to toss out of the union any men causing disturbances.

As an incentive to stay away from the bars, the city government arranged for strikers to play indoor baseball at the city's armory. Such "wholesome amusement" during the afternoons would provide the men with exercise and keep them off the street and presumably out of trouble.[26] As the strike wore on, the results of the stringent liquor prohibition endorsed by Ellis, the city tavern league, and the labor unions bore fruit. Arrests for drunk and disorderly conduct fell by more than 33 percent during the summer, especially those that usually took place on Sunday night or Monday morning.[27]

But precautionary measures and injunctions to remain orderly did not prevent sporadic violence from erupting during the week of April 19, despite the fact that is was the Christian Holy week. On Maundy Thursday, one of the nonstriking workmen who had just left the John Widdicomb Company factory was said to have insulted a woman bystander with "questionable" remarks. A crowd of more than 200 men and women gathered around the alleged offender, beating and jostling him and hitting him with a club. Meanwhile, at the Gunn furniture plant, a crowd greeted one of the nonstriking workers with a shower of stones. Down the street, two union pickets rescued several nonstriking workers who were assaulted as they left the Widdicomb Furniture Company factory. A fourth clash took place at the Imperial factory near Broadway. The next day, Good Friday, more violence occurred back at the John Widdicomb factory. These outbursts so alarmed local saloon owners that their begrudging endorsement turned into wholehearted compliance with the city's resolution for closing bars in the morning.[28]

Several Easter Sunday sermons addressed the growing tensions by urging arbitration. Perhaps the churches could succeed in bringing reconciliation where the city government had failed. After all, peace would be assured "if men who have differences would only lay before the Lord Jesus the questions which perplex them." But the violence resumed after Easter, and conflicts continued throughout the strike-torn summer, many of them incited by Polish workers, who were arrested in increasing numbers for rioting and "assault" at various factory sites surrounding their homes. Generally far more inclined to confront strikebreakers with violence than any other ethnic groups among the strikers, the Poles were the most radical of all the city's workers.[29]

Given the persistent violence, it is no wonder that newspaper rumors about Big Bill Haywood coming to town stirred concern that gunplay and worse might erupt on the West Side, where "trouble is most likely to break out" among the "many Lithuanian and Polish members of unions in this district." Haywood, the leader of the radical Industrial Workers of the World (IWW), advocated "one big union" of all workers against capitalist society. Involved with organizing western miners, northern loggers, and various railroad workers, he had seen a great deal of armed conflict in his labor career. In anticipation of his arrival, newspapers reported factory owners had started to recruit armed guards for their plants.[30]

The threat of a private army financed by the manufacturers evaporated when Mayor Ellis and Kent County Sheriff William J. Hurley refused to issue permits for arming additional auxiliary protection. As private enterprises, the furniture companies had no power to deputize men unless requested to do so by the police and, for now, that was not going to happen. Neither the city nor the county would be responsible for escalating the conflict or surrendering their legal prerogatives. Hoping to defuse the mounting tensions, Ellis reiterated his pledge to keep the manufacturers from hiring armed guards. Saloon owners publicly endorsed the strikers' goals while they advocated the need for abstinence and began policing the customers inside their establishments even as union pickets policed outside the bars.[31]

Meanwhile, striking workers gained small advances. Three of the smaller factories agreed to the union demands without any formal recognition of the union. The Muriel, the Veit, and the Interchangeable companies, respectively, agreed to increase wages, reduce hours, and eliminate piece rates. But the total number of men affected by these settlements was fewer than 100, a fraction of the total workforce that remained out on strike. More important, from the employers' perspective, none of the three firms belonged to the FMA. Anticipating second thoughts among its members and working to strengthen its ranks, the FMA leadership met and voted to refuse any form of arbitration and to expel any member who dared to engage in the process.[32]

A Hot, Dry Summer

By the end of April, with the strike at full strength and no resolution in sight, it was obvious that a hot and "dry" — in every sense of the word — summer loomed over Grand Rapids. Ellis's city government officially assumed a neutral stance in the proceedings, but remained clearly inclined to favor the workers, a position that helped reduce some of the tensions that had steadily built up in the early weeks of the strike. As the walkout wore on, the voters' good will toward the mayor and his personal assurances of working for their interests paid off time and again as Ellis interceded to calm angry crowds.

On April 24, for example, more than 200 men, women, and children gathered outside the Michigan Chair Company hoping to intimidate anyone who might want to break ranks with the strikers and return to work. Company manager Thomas Garratt drove up to the factory gates, waved his fist and shouted at the crowd that he was going to keep an open shop and that no-body could dictate labor policy to him! Ellis appeared a few minutes later, addressed the crowd, and made a show of talking with Garratt in a friendly, relaxed manner. The mayor then asked everyone to disperse. More than half the people went home while the rest remained to speak with the mayor and shake his hand.[33]

Three days later, the newspapers printed the contents of a circular that evidently had been sent around the city by the manufacturers. Endorsed by J. S. Linton, secretary of the National Association of Manufacturers, the pamphlet exaggerated both the demands and the numbers of Grand Rapids employees, placing the fault for the strike on outside union agitators. According to the circular, the FMA performed a vital service as the bulwark of resistance to labor radicalism. Unless stopped in Grand Rapids, unionization of the furniture industry would "sweep across the nation" and affect "every community engaged in this manufacture."[34] The episode showed that the strike no longer concerned only local men and local conditions. What had begun as a community imbroglio had become of interest to outsiders. Big labor lined up behind the workers and big business lined up behind the factory owners, each claiming that the future of American life rode on the outcome of this contest.

One day after the circular was published, O. H. L. Wernicke, head of the

Macey Company, delivered a blustery ultimatum to Mayor Ellis demanding police protection for those who were still working in the city's factories. Despite
quiet in the streets for more than a week, Wernicke — and evidently others —
feared violent confrontation. Additionally, Wernicke argued that the city government was responsible for any damages sustained at factories in the course of
the labor dispute. Wernicke made it plain that the industrialists viewed Ellis and
his administration as their enemy and would go outside the city in search of assistance. He could not understand why the city tolerated the string of pickets
outside the gates at his own and other factories. Unless the men were removed,
the factory owners would be obliged "in self-defense to obtain such aid and
protection through such lawful sources as are open to us."[35]

As the manufacturers' line hardened, so, too, did public opinion against
them. The *Creston News* praised the workers' restraint in the past and damned
the manufacturers as fear mongers, who, "unused to strikes, have been alarmed
every time a stone was thrown and have magnified the act of some small boy
into a riot." The paper's editor doubted if the citizens committee, meeting all
through the strike's first weeks, might be capable of impartial judgment. Although the committee continued to gather information, take depositions from
workers, and investigate marketplace conditions, the conclusions would be suspect, for three of its members were "by association, education, occupation and
instinct absolutely warped on the side of the employers."[36]

During the last weeks of April, newspapers released the citizens committee's
preliminary findings, which created little hope for any significant breakthrough.
Taking a middle ground, the committee called for an eight-hour day and minor
wage adjustments while recognizing the manufacturers' claims that they did not
dominate the national furniture market. More than that, noted the committee,
the Grand Rapids industrialists stood at a distinct disadvantage when it came to
national freight rates. Concessions made by railroads in March applied only to
western markets, not to the more lucrative eastern ones.[37]

As the committee issued its report, Mayor Ellis visited the Macey Company
where, despite Wernicke's fears, all was quiet. Meanwhile, the *Evening Press* endorsed the committee's findings. Conceding that Grand Rapids' share of the
national marketplace was healthy but by no means overwhelming, the *Press*
urged modification of wage demands on the part of workers and acceptance of
fewer hours by the owners. "The welfare of society, as well as economic production, is dependent upon the vitality of the workers," said the paper, and
"the happiness of the homes and well being of the family are affected by the
hours of labor." Certainly the factory owners ought to see some justice in acced-
ing to a few of the workers' demands; the unwholesome effects of difficult
working conditions far outweighed the advantages of production.[38]

If figuring out whose side had the greater merit remained difficult inside
Grand Rapids, then following the story outside the city was even more complicated. At first, little mention of the strike appeared in state and regional news-

papers or those located in the nation's major cities. The most detailed coverage came from the *Detroit Free Press.* Announcing, with some overstatement, that 59 firms had been forced to a complete halt by a walkout of the city's 6,000 furniture workers, the *Free Press* noted that police protection against the strikers remained the industrialists' chief concern. Playing on the incipient threat of violence in Grand Rapids, the Detroit paper lamented the recent abolition of the state's labor arbitration board, which might have served some real purpose for a city whose "bread and butter" was jeopardized.[39]

Allowing that it was difficult to know actual conditions in the plants and how legitimate the FMA's claims were "owing to the scrupulously maintained secrecy of the manufacturers," the *Free Press* concluded "that from a look at the state census figures…the workers were indeed the injured party." The newspaper calculated that the Grand Rapids furniture industry had jumped from $9.5 million in revenue in 1909 to $11.5 million in 1910 and was clearly in a position to grant higher wages. The paper also noted that a recent reciprocity treaty with Canada added a great, untapped market for the furniture makers without fear of tariffs.[40]

Across Lake Michigan, the *Milwaukee Journal* carried occasional paragraphs about the start of the strike and the sporadic conflicts between strikers and strikebreakers. Elsewhere, the *New York Times,* the *New York Sun* and the *Atlanta Constitution* merely noted that a strike had begun in Grand Rapids furniture factories over wages and hours. After these initial notices, news of the strike virtually disappeared from outside newspapers, leaving the furniture manufacturers to present their side in trade journals and allied commercial publications without rebuttal. Over time, while receiving strong support from local editorials, the striking workers would become increasingly isolated from outside coverage.[41]

Early in May, the city's principal trade union newspaper, the *Observer,* declared that in light of the strong public support for the strikers, "the manufacturers face defeat." Echoing the *Creston News,* the *Observer* called the citizens committee a "waste of time" given that any group of experts was capable of doctoring up statistics "to fit every side of the question."[42] The will of the people would be heard, said the *Observer,* and the truth was plain enough to see.

The *Evening News* joined the chorus of support for the workers, asserting that, even with a 10 percent wage increase, the average wage earner took home "less than the city of Detroit pays per day to newly arrived Polish and Italian immigrants for work on the streets and sewers." The *Evening News* went on to attack the manufacturers as simply too cheap, claiming their short-sighted penny pinching inhibited the wealth of the city by reducing the flow of money all the way around. The strikers' demands were "remarkably reasonable," said the *News,* while the industrialists sought privilege at the expense of ordinary citizens. Such an attitude deserved a slap across the wrist, if nothing else. Later, when the police commissioner was compelled to resign after ignoring the mayor's call to keep the Peninsular Club closed on Sundays, the *Evening News* applauded: Special treatment should not be accorded to the people who seemed bent on taking from the city without giving back to it.[43]

Religious Undercurrents

Early May continued to bring support for the workers from a variety of sources, chiefly from unofficial reports by Bishop Schrembs about the findings of recent citizens committee meetings. Citing "what the inquiry revealed and did not reveal" to the general public, Schrembs advocated "arbitration instead of starvation." He described the terrible living conditions and meager wages of the majority of furniture workers, stating that as a resident and pastor in the city since 1900, he had ample opportunities to become familiar with the city's Catholic residents, and he based his opinions on personal observations and experience. "I consider the present labor situation in our city as a most deplorable one from every point of view." He would "welcome and hasten the day when compulsory arbitration will force men dealing with their fellow men to let fairness and justice come to their own through reasonable methods rather than through the cowering of men's hearts through the cruel pangs of hunger of their wives and children."[44]

Schrembs's views reflected the official papal position on labor matters as expressed in Leo XIII's 1891 papal bull *Rerum Novarum* — that the consolidation of labor was an equitable response to the concentration of capital.[45] The Catholic position and the one espoused by the city's newspapers reinforced each other, both arguing for social justice by creating a balance of economic interests in a capitalist society. The bishop expressed his support for labor at a mass meeting on May 3, where he spoke to 2,500 strikers at the Ramona Theater. The *Evening Press* described deafening applause as Schrembs praised the workers' moderation and restraint, noting that "had it not been for the labor unions, we would still have the conditions which shamed men and women one or two generations ago."[46]

This one-sided interpretation of events did not last long. Openly voicing disappointment in the bishop for speaking out, Reverend Wishart said it had been his impression that none of the committee members would publicly comment on the committee's findings or conduct their own "personal interviews." Wishart noted that while he chose not to speak right away, "I may have something to say on points not covered in the report" at a later date, and he implied that Schrembs had violated a sacred trust placed with him by the FMA and city government.[47] Responding to the minister's charges, Schrembs denied that he had violated any confidentiality and asserted that he spoke to address the FMA's resistance to any form of collective negotiation, "a condition of unreasonable egotism which threatens the best interest of the entire city."[48]

With broad support from the Catholic hierarchy, city officials, and newspaper editors, it seemed only a matter of time before the strikers would win some concessions from the manufacturers. Such a conclusion appeared further warranted when five more non-FMA firms moved toward tentative settlement with their employees. The options presented were for an increase in wages matched by a ten-hour workday, or no wage increase and a reduction to nine hours daily. The fact that these companies collectively employed fewer than 400 workers did not matter as much as the hope their action offered that the strike would soon be over. A meeting between representatives of the strikers and factory owners took place on May 6, helping buoy such cautious optimism.[49]

At the same time, new undercurrents appeared as the strike affected the various ethnic and religious groups in Grand Rapids. The conservative Dutch Reformed community on the south side of the city chartered the Grandville Avenue Dutch Labor Society without indicating whether the society was pro- or anti-union, merely that it was "largely religious in its aims." This was a subtle but dramatic step away from the Reformed Church's earlier reticence and at times open hostility to dealing with secular matters. The *Evening Press* carried a story about the labor society, emphasizing that the organization's chief assumptions revolved around the belief that "there is no problem which cannot be solved by the application of Christian principles."[50]

This resurgent appeal to religious foundations as the way to solve social problems promised some results. After all, both Catholic Bishop Schrembs and the Calvinist Dutch labor society placed their faith in Christian principles to solve the thorny dilemma posed by inequitable economic conditions. However, the question remained whether these principles would prove strong enough to surmount strong ethnic divisions, even assuming that everybody agreed upon what "Christian principles" meant. Baptist minister Wishart could rightfully claim to represent an interpretation of "Christian principles," but he had opposed the strike from the outset. Bishop Schrembs laid claim to the same principles while supporting the workers. Throughout the strike, the search for common religious ground proved to be as futile as efforts to use the city government as a vehicle for arbitration.

The Gathering Storm

By mid-May, the continued stalemate created a climate where the desire for some sort of action became paramount. Tensions grew as rumors spread throughout the city. One such rumor had it that a small army of strikebreakers was en route from Chicago. The local *Observer* reported that this private force would lift the siege of the city's factories by discrediting the strikers, luring them into saloons, and getting them intoxicated. After that, the paper charged, these provocateurs would push the drunken men into some rash action, perhaps inciting them to violence or returning to work.[51]

Nothing came of the threat, despite the fact that 300 men from Chicago did show up in Grand Rapids, stayed overnight in a converted piano factory, refused to work once they learned they had been brought in as strikebreakers, and left the next day.[52] The FMA never issued a statement explaining who brought the men to town, why, or what happened. Their appearance remained a mystery, but it did serve to fuel suspicion about how far the manufacturers might go to crush the strikers.

Even as Grand Rapids briefly lodged the 300 reluctant strikebreakers, Chicago was hosting the National Association of Furniture Manufacturers. One topic of conversation was the general slump in the marketplace and industrial slowdowns across the nation. Another topic was the strike in Grand Rapids. O. H. L. Wernicke of the Macey Company spoke extemporaneously to the banquet guests, lashing out against unions and insisting on the need to preserve the open shop.

The *Evening News* reported on both the national conference and Wernicke's remarks, supplementing its coverage with some original research on the furniture industry in Grand Rapids. While it was true that as a whole the Grand Rapids furniture factories did not dominate the entire national marketplace, the *News* reported, six local companies accounted for one-third of the national production of certain specialized goods such as bedroom suites. In their respective product and price-range niches, Nelson-Matter, Berkey & Gay, Royal Furniture, Oriel, Phoenix and Sligh each exercised significant influence across the United States.

The paper's investigations also revealed that local workers did indeed receive less money for more labor than elsewhere. A member of the national association, Lyman Lathrop, speaking confidentially to the newspaper reporter at the conference, confirmed that Grand Rapids industrialists got "a higher grade of labor at a price rather below that paid in other furniture centers....In no place in the country do they work their men ten hours a day, except possibly in some of the southern centers, and I am told that the South is the only part of the country where wages are as low as they are in Grand Rapids."[53]

Immediately after Lathrop's words appeared in print, the Reverend Wishart spoke out against the strikers. Referring to an incident two days earlier when 100 nonstrikers barricaded themselves in the Show Case plant to fend off a large crowd of strikers, the Baptist minister asserted that conditions were "fast moving" to a state where "citizens will demand the enforcement of the law. The gathering crowds around a factory and threatening men who want to work there is unlawful." Alluding to the possibilities of bringing in the Pinkertons or other private police forces, Wishart declared, "If the city authorities do not disperse the crowds, other means must be used to preserve order. Politics may let confusion go on for a while, but politics will have to get out of the way."[54]

Reports of Wishart's attack on Ellis and the city's earlier denial of special protection for Wernicke's Macey Company factory were published in the industrialists' national journal, the *Furniture Manufacturer and Artisan,* a part of the manufacturers' continued call for sympathy outside the city. Hometown folks, few of whom read the publication, continued to feel that the strikers were being wronged and that their employers were slandering and misrepresenting the workers' cause.

Increasingly frustrated by the FMA's resistance to compromise even though there was strong local support for their cause, furniture workers and their families grew anxious for some return to a "normal" routine of work and income. All through the second week in May, crowds gathered around West Side factories. Despite the lack of violence, the frequency of the gatherings and the growing numbers of people gave rise to uneasiness in the city. The manufacturers as a group would not concede anything to the workers despite mounting support for the workers' claims. While Mayor Ellis and his newly appointed police commissioner, John Timmer, both felt that union pickets served to maintain order rather than disrupt it, the manufacturers declared that the union pickets attracted menacing crowds. Drawn out of curiosity or idleness, the crowds harassed nonstriking workers trying to enter the picketed plants. For the factory owners, union pickets represented a threat to their loyal employees. Voicing their dissatisfaction through a new organization they dubbed the Grand Rapids Citizens Alliance, factory owners circulated petitions backing Wernicke's demands for increased numbers of police officers and removal of the union pickets.[55]

Spokesman for the Alliance, attorney Stuart E. Knappen argued that large numbers of men who wanted to work were effectively kept away from their labors through sheer intimidation. "We believe that it is self-evident that the best interests of the community require that every man who is willing to work should be employed," declaimed Knappen. "Law and order must be maintained in this community."[56] Knappen argued that determining working conditions and setting wage levels were matters best left to the private sector. The role of government was to police the marketplace, making it safe for entrepreneurs and industrial capitalism. Disruption must be suppressed at all costs. To side with the workers only violated government's chief function.

Knappen appeared to be distorting Ellis's role and overstating the threat represented by the pickets. Mayor Ellis made nearly daily visits to the factory sites, talked with the union pickets and found their behavior orderly, their appearance proper. Despite a warm-up in the weather, the pickets wore derby hats, coats, and ties. They carried no signs or brickbats to distinguish themselves as strikers; eventually they simply wore small identification badges in their lapels.

In early May, another small factory, the Fritz Furniture Company, settled with its employees, conceding to every demand except union recognition. Hopes among the striking workers rose even higher when newspaper reports circulated that Charles R. Sligh, owner of the large plant bearing his name, considered withdrawing from the FMA in order to settle with his men.[57] If the papers were to be believed, serious breaches existed in the ranks of the FMA, and the piecemeal settlements among the lesser factories were precursors to an eventual citywide accord.

Despite Ellis's efforts to keep a lid on the tense situation, a series of episodes in mid-May demonstrated that potential for violence lay just below the surface. On the evening of May 12, an employee of the American Seating Company stood by the factory door waving a long target pistol while shouting at the gathered crowd to leave. "The attitude of the man and his orders to the crowd angered peaceable men," reported the *Evening News,* and as soon as he tried to depart, hundreds of women and children surrounded him and then hounded him down the street. A policeman tried to break up the crowd but failed to do so; one report stated many non-English-speaking immigrants at the scene failed to understand the officer's command to disperse.[58] At the same time, not far away, another more violent episode took place. Harry Widdicomb, who had become head of the John Widdicomb Company when his father died in 1910, had begun to shepherd loyal workers to and from the plant in his own car. One worker had missed his accustomed ride and was assaulted as he tried to walk home after the day's work.[59]

Commenting on the confrontation with the gun-waving worker, the newspapers were more concerned with the crowd's composition than with the actual violence; the *Evening News* worried that too many children were mixed in with the adults and might be injured if any serious activity occurred. A photograph dominating the front page bore the caption "the danger in the strike zone," and the accompanying news story reported crowd numbers exceeding 200. The entire factory neighborhood housed immigrant families, densely packed in small homes and tiny yards. Homes adjacent to the factories were "chiefly occupied by foreigners" and were so thickly settled that "if men merely step into their own yards a crowd is a result." Crowds seemed less restrained or subject to control by the pickets or police when compared to other neighborhoods in the city, the paper noted, and large numbers of women and children in a sportive temper mingled with men "in an ugly mood" to create problems of control.[60]

Two days later, the *Evening News* presented city readers with a report on a piece of propaganda circulated by the FMA to the National Association of Furniture Manufacturers. The new FMA pamphlet announced three important points to fellow businessmen around the country. First, the mayor of Grand Rapids had not served the city's best interest by using his authority to negotiate with five factories unaffiliated with the FMA. Public officials had no right interfering in the marketplace, according to this account, a sentiment consistent with the industrialists' view that labor conditions and wages were a "private" matter between employer and employee. Second, the FMA asserted that most of the city's factories still operated at a 40 percent capacity, more than enough to produce goods in time for the June buyers show in Grand Rapids. Symbolically, the trade show would test whether the manufacturers could outlast the strikers and successfully meet the demands of the national marketplace. Third, and most offensive to the workers, was a baseless assertion that the manufacturers had broken the strike and that work would resume on a regular basis beginning Monday, May 15.

That Monday became doubly important when the Show Case Company publicly announced that it had subcontracted more than $50,000 worth of work outside the Grand Rapids area to ensure enough samples for the summer buyers show. Company treasurer Samuel Young sarcastically quipped to a local reporter, "Yes, we rather hate to place our work outside of the city, but I guess the boys here don't want to work." Continuing in the same vein, he remarked that the laborers here evidently "want a little vacation and I guess we will let them have one."[61]

Young's bravado and taunting belied the reality of continuing negotiations among several of the city's firms and their workers. Along with the six recently settled companies, the Nachtegall Company had started to make settlement overtures to its workers, despite threats of expulsion from the FMA. Given these developments, there could be little doubt that the building tensions might explode. Incensed by Young's insulting comments, the strikers remained strong, and each day additional nonstrikers joined their ranks.

Newspapers on Monday, May 15, carried Young's words around the city along with the FMA's unilateral declaration that work would resume among the "broken" strikers. That night, striking workers and their supporters made sure the manufacturers learned firsthand about the strikers' resolve not to back down and would think twice before blustering along about "the boys" wanting a "vacation."

Endnotes

1. Viva Flaherty, "History of the Strike," pp. 9-10; *Evening Press,* January 22, 1910, p. 7; July 26, 1910, p. 8.
2. Z. Z. Lydens, *The Story of Grand Rapids,* pp. 355-56.
3. *News* and *Press,* March 1, 1911, p. 1.
4. Ibid.
5. *News* and *Press,* March 2, 1911, p. 1.
6. *News,* March 6, 1911, p. 4.
7. Ibid.
8. *Press,* March 13, 1911, p. 2.
9. *News,* March 15, 1911, p. 4.
10. *Press,* March 17, 1911, p. 13.
11. *News* and *Press,* March 23, 1911, p. 1.
12. *News,* March 24, 1911, p. 10; March 25, 1911, p. 1.
13. *News,* March 26, 1911, pp. 1, 4, 12; *Press,* March 27, 1911, pp. 1, 3.
14. *Press,* March 28, 1911, p. 1.
15. *Furniture Manufacturer and Artisan,* April, 1911, p. 163.
16. *Press,* March 30, 1911, p. 4.
17. *Furniture Manufacturer and Artisan,* April, 1911, p. 163.

18. *Creston News,* March 31, 1911, p. 2.

19. *Press,* April 3, 1911, pp. 1-6; *Herald,* April 2, p. 1; April 3, p. 1.

20. *Herald,* April 11, p. 12.

21. *Creston News,* April 14, p. 2.

22. *Press,* April 17, p. 1.

23. *News,* April 19, 1911, p. 1.

24. Ibid. p. 12; April 20, 1911, p. 1.

25. *Press,* April 20, 1911, p. 10.

26. *News,* April 21, 1911, p. 2.

27. *Press,* June 29, 1911, p. 1; June 6, 1911, p. 1.

28. *News,* April 21, 1911, p. 19; April 22, 1911, p. 11; *Press,* April 22, 1911, p. 11.

29. Ibid. April 24, 1911, p. 2; *Press,* April 21, 1911, p. 1.

30. *News,* April 24, 1911, p. 1; April 22, 1911, p. 3.

31. *Press,* April 25, 1911, p. 9; April 24, 1911, p. 1.

32. *Press* April 24, 1911, p. 1; News, April 25, 1911, p. 1.

33. Ibid.

34. *Press,* April 27, 1911, pp. 1, 4.

35. *News,* April 28, 1911, p. 1.

36. *Creston News,* April 28, 1911, p. 2.

37. *News,* April 29, 1911, p. 1.

38. *Press,* April 29, 1911, p. 11.

39. *Detroit Free Press,* April 20, 1911, p. 3; April 25, 1911, p. 3.

40. Ibid. April 20, 1911, pp. 3-4.

41. *Milwaukee Journal,* April 21, 1911, p. 1; the reports referred to were taken from a sampling of major regional newspapers in the United States for the months of April through August, 1911.

42. *Observer,* May 1, 1911, p. 2.

43. *News,* May 1, 1911, p. 4; May 2, 1911, p. 6.

44. *Press,* May 3, p. 12.

45. Aaron I. Abell, "American Catholic Response to Industrial Conflict: The Arbital Process 1885-1900," *The Catholic Historical Review* XLVI, no. 4 (January, 1956), pp. 385- 407.

46. *Press,* May 4, 1911, p. 11.

47. Ibid.

48. *News,* May 5, 1911, p. 1.

49. Ibid. May 6, 1911, p. 1.

50. *Press,* May 8, 1911, pp. 2, 9.

51. *Observer,* May 8, 1911, p. 1.

52. *News,* May 9, 1911, p. 1; Press, May 9, p. 11.

53. *News,* May 10, 1911, p. 1, 8.

54. *Press,* May 11, 1911, p. 1.

55. Ibid. May 11, 1911, p. 10; May 12, 1911, pp. 1, 3, 6; *News,* May 12, 1911, p. 3.

56. *Press,* May 8, 1911, p. 9.

57. *Detroit Free Press,* May 12, 1911, p. 6.

58. *News,* May 13, 1911, p. 11.

59. Ibid. May 16, 1911, p. 1.

60. *Press,* May 13, 1911, pp. 1-2.

61. Ibid. p. 1; May 15, 1911, pp. 1, 8.

Leaders and Scenes of the Strike

There are few photographs of action during the furniture strike. The best historical documents are these grainy images and cutlines from the weekly newspaper, Grit. *Unfortunately, the original images no longer exist. (GRPL, 185-1-75)*

POLICE LOADING GUNS PREPARATORY TO SHOOTING AT MOB.

GRAND RAPIDS POLICEMEN WITH GUNS DRAWN, DRIVING OFF PICKETS.

LEADERS OF GRAND RAPIDS STRIKE. ORGANIZER HYLE IN THE CENTER.

POLICE GUARDING STRIKEBREAKERS TAKEN TO FACTORY IN MOTOR CAR.

POLICE SHOOTING INTO MOB OF STRIKERS. A REMARKABLE SNAPSHOT

The John Widdicomb Company's Fifth Street factory on the West Side was the scene of a confrontation involving strikers, strikebreakers, and police. (GRPL, 54-48-2)

Strikers had supporters in many parts of the community. Here one of the union leaders, Gerrit Verberg (right), and an unidentified colleague pose in front of a sign at the Lyric vaudeville theater announcing that its morning receipts would be donated to the strikers each day. (GRPL, 185-1-75)

Viva Flaherty was not a strike leader, but one of its strongest supporters. In its aftermath she wrote a short history of the event that was strongly critical of the Rev. Alfred Wishart. (GRPL, Central High School Yearbook, 1903)

Chapter 5

Riot and Reaction:
The Failure of Class-Based Action

The escalating war of words over the weekend of May 13 and 14 challenged striking workers and their families to respond to the FMA's claim that the strike was broken and that production would resume "as normal" on Monday, May 15. The response came that evening on the West Side, along Davis Avenue and Fifth Street, where an estimated 1,200 men, women, and children had gathered in the vicinity of the Widdicomb and the John Widdicomb factories. The frustration that had been simmering for many weeks finally boiled over into violence as the crowd rioted, showering nonstriking workers with stones and successfully resisting the efforts of police and fire companies to restore order. By midnight, the unruly throng had grown to more than 2,000 individuals who filled the narrow streets, retreating only after pistol shots were fired.

The incident convinced manufacturers that they could not trust city government to safeguard their factories or protect replacement workers. Determined to hold firm in the aftermath of the violence, they turned to county authorities and private sources to guarantee law and order. Even more ominously, the confrontation hardened each side's will, removing all possibility of a negotiated settlement. It now seemed clear to both sides that the strike's end would come only with organized labor's collapse or the FMA's capitulation.

A Night of Unrest

According to the *Evening News,* the West Side riot actually encompassed a series of smaller, roving incidents that converged into a single, large-scale fracas. The first of the incidents came at around 5:30 p.m. when Harry Widdicomb, head of the John Widdicomb Company, drove his car through the crowd surrounding his factory to pick up some of his nonstriking employees and drive them home, a tactic he had adopted from the strike's outset. When

Widdicomb tried to drive out of the factory gate, he encountered an angry fusillade of words and then an attack on his car.

Women, some with children in their arms, formed the front ranks of the rioters, creating a wall around the car, behind which men gathered to throw sticks, stones, and whatever else was handy. When no more rocks or bricks could be found, some women were reported to have offered their shoes. According to another account, pistol shots were heard at one point, but the crowd was undeterred in its push toward the factory gates. For a time, emotions were said to have run so deeply that when police arrived, one mother put down her child to pick up a club and wield it against one of the officers. It was not lost on the reporter that the woman was dressed "in the style of the typical Polish foreigner" or that the violence had erupted in a predominantly Polish neighborhood.

As incidents continued into the evening, more and more people poured into the area around the Widdicomb factories. Fire engines showed up about an hour after the melee had started, turning their hoses on the rioters in hopes of breaking up the crowd. After ten minutes of unsuccessful efforts, the engines returned to their respective firehouses. Still trapped behind the factory gates, Harry Widdicomb tried to break through by retreating to his car, now guarded by three policemen, and drive out into the street. Once they spotted him, rioters pressed forward to keep him in the factory confines, again tossing stones and other debris, retreating only when the policemen drew their pistols. Then Mayor Ellis arrived, hoping that a personal plea to the rioters would quiet the outbreak. Ellis's popularity on the West Side and previous successes with direct pleas influenced his decision to address the crowd personally.

Ellis's appearance elicited cheers as he walked through the densely packed streets and into the factory. After conferring with Harry Widdicomb, he returned outside, raised his hands in a call for silence, and "the crowd came forward, like an orderly audience." One man shouted, "We'll believe Ellis anytime, but we won't let these 'coppers' come around here bossing us." Faced with a receptive, apparently disciplined although still angry crowd, Ellis pleaded for peace, and some in the crowd drifted away. During this brief lull, Harry Widdicomb and five workmen passengers made their escape under an escort of policemen who rode on the car's running boards with guns drawn.

But the disturbance was far from over. No sooner had Ellis departed than the protesters began drifting back, intent on renewing pressure against Harry Widdicomb. As darkness fell, rioters lined the north and south sides of the streets to begin a systematic stone bombardment of the John Widdicomb factory. A solitary policeman at the factory gates fingered his pistol, but as long as the attacks centered on property rather than people, he remained still. He continued to stand at his post while the crowd hurled stones at the factory, breaking every window in the place. Finally, thirty club-wielding policemen pushed forward, breaking up the crowd and falling upon one stubborn protester who re-fused to leave.[1]

Midway through the efforts to disperse the rioters, the police arrested a few men and began to retreat towards the Sixth Street Bridge. Using their prisoners as shields, the policemen fired their weapons into the air until they ran out of ammunition. Hand-to-hand battles ensued and the rioters threatened to over-whelm the police until reinforcements appeared. The fighting continued until "the street was filled with madly running and cursing men and women" with "almost every other face...streaked with blood from an injury or from the injury of another."

During this bloody encounter, Mayor Ellis appeared on the West Side for the second time, accompanying the police reserves, and once more urged the throng to disperse. The crowd cheered but refused to leave. After Ellis departed, fire engines again arrived to hose down the crowd. According to one report, "Hundreds were drenched, but they retreated reluctantly and their mood was ugly."[2]

The Morning After

The morning after the West Side riot, all the daily papers carried accounts of the evening's violence. More and more details became public knowledge as re-porters on the scene followed up their initial accounts with further investigation of the unprecedented confrontation. The *Evening News* called the incident "anarchy pure and simple" and called for increased police enforcement to con-trol this "intolerable situation." The *Press* gave a more detailed account, in-cluding two front-page photographs and emphasizing the "pistol battle" that the *Evening News* failed to mention. More than any other paper in town, the *Press* focused on the Polish character of the neighborhood and the degree of violence that took place. Four unnamed men were reported to have been arrested: two Poles, a Lithuanian, and an American-born resident. The American-born indi-vidual refused to leave the scene after the police reinforcements arrived, where-upon, the *Press* reported, four policemen clubbed him into submission. He was the only official casualty noted in the newspapers. The three immigrants who were arrested did not work at the Widdicomb factory; their involvement appar-ently had more to do with the fact that they already were home rather than an unwillingness to go home.

In a proclamation written in English and Polish and issued the next morning, Mayor Ellis urged restrained behavior, obedience to the law, and respect for private property. The proclamation also took particular note of the role played by women and children in the riots, stating, "This is public notice that women and children take their chances if they congregate at factories and they must keep away or accept the results as the streets will be cleared."[3]

The *Press* incorrectly blamed both Harry and William Widdicomb for prompting the violence – Harry for his refusal to shut down his factory for the duration of the strike as his brother William had done, and William for brandishing a gun on several occasions in the week before the riot. (Actually, it was Harry who had brandished the pistol.) The *Press* also printed a letter to the editor blaming both the Widdicombs and Reverend Wishart for inciting workers to violence. The author, identified only as "A Business Woman," derided Wishart's claims to have the best interests of the workingman at heart, asking rhetorically when had he decided to join the masses? For if he had, then he could learn of "the conditions of bending every energy of mind, soul and body over a whirring machine for ten hours, five and a half days a week...with the complacent hope that when he reaches the height of skill, he will be able to command $12 per week."[4]

Outside the city, Kent County Sheriff Hurley voiced the hostility that the manufacturers felt towards the municipal government when he said, "What is needed is to take Mayor Ellis by the nape of the neck and the seat of his pants and throw him off the board of police" so that the strikers could be handled in an appropriate fashion. After the strike was over, this desire to separate the mayor from any further exercise of civil power would find fullest expression in a 1916 reform movement to change the city charter, but for now the anti-Ellis sentiment remained embodied in angry words about his lax attitude towards dangerous people.

Hurley also complained about members of the police and fire departments who had been reluctant to take action against the rioting strikers. Newspaper reporters looking into the actions of the fire department during the May 15 riot found that training the water hoses on the crowd had not been a well-received command. Two senior firemen had been dismissed shortly after the riot for challenging the order to hose down the crowd and threatening to cut the hoses with fire axes to keep the order from being carried out.[5] Part of their reluctance to use the fire hoses stemmed from the presence of women and children in the crowd, a stance hardliners found objectionable.

The Peace Patrols

In the face of calls for sterner action, and with gun sales reportedly increased across the city, Mayor Ellis hit upon an unusual strategy for maintaining order. Shortly after the riot, he called for a special police force made up of strikers to patrol the factory districts. Armed only with nightsticks and recruited from among the ranks of the strikers themselves, the "peace patrol" numbered nearly 100 men, a significant number of them Dutch. By manning the patrol with strikers, Ellis not only empowered workingmen from the factory districts, but the wages paid by the city supplemented the meager strike benefits accorded by the union.[6] Employing the Dutch-dominated patrols to keep the peace allowed Ellis to extend municipal authority, and moneys, without engendering criticism from the community, which continued to support the strikers.

The novelty of using workers to quell strike-centered violence won praise across the country. An editorial in the national journal *Outlook* defended labor unions in general against the charges of unwarranted violence and pointed in particular to the success of the Grand Rapids peace patrols in reducing factory-district violence. "Thus it happens that men on strike are helping to guard the factories in which they have refused to work and check the disorder of irresponsible sympathizers," noted the journal. "Such working men show themselves not only good citizens whose patriotism takes a practical form, but also the wisest kind of advocates for advancing the cause of the wage earner."[7]

To no one's surprise, the furniture manufacturers did not share the positive assessment of the peace patrols. Harshly critical of Ellis in their trade journals, they moved their battle into the courtroom, where their attorneys, McGeorge Bundy and Francis Campau, argued that the presence of union pickets outside the various factories had prompted the Monday night violence.[8] Seeking a restraining order to keep the strikers and their families away, the manufacturers also submitted forty affidavits to prove that they had been placed in a vulnerable position by Ellis's "hostile" attitude towards them.[9] The National Association of Manufacturers joined them on the rhetorical front when NAM President John Kirby, Jr., roundly condemned the union, the strike, and the violence by writing that "the American Federation of Labor is engaged in open warfare on Jesus Christ and his principles, and I challenge the federation to disprove my assertion."

A hearing for a permanent injunction against the union pickets was scheduled for the end of May. Meanwhile, according to the newspapers, the mayor's peace patrols achieved significant results in reducing threats of disorder. Unfortunately for the workers' cause, however, the makeup of the patrols reflected a deeper set of ethnic divisions that would plague the strike. The Dutch and American-born workers in the patrols greatly outnumbered their Polish and Lithuanian counterparts, who were generally more radical and more prone to violence than their Dutch colleagues.

Dutch workers were also troubled by the possibility that the strike was contrary to their church's teachings. As the weeks wore on, the Christian Reformed Church began to investigate whether church member participation in the United Brotherhood of Carpenters and Joiners was compatible with church doctrine. The western classis, the regional governing body for area Christian Reformed churches, convened a panel to explore the union's oaths, rituals, and activities. Any decisions handed down by the classis could have serious consequences for organized labor in Grand Rapids.

Just as those enforcing restraint had little in common with the strike's most outspoken leaders, there were profound differences within the strikers' ranks about how best to handle the strike. The resulting fractures among the workmen, along with dwindling economic resources, spelled serious limitations for the strikers and an important advantage for the manufacturers.[10]

Charges and Countercharges

While waiting for court action on the FMA's request for a permanent injunction against the picketers, the pages of the city's newspapers again became a battleground. In a bitter complaint, Bishop Schrembs accused the FMA of hiring private detectives to trail him. The nine-hour day, not personalities, stood at the heart of the dispute, he argued, charging that the factory owners had created the issue of unionization as a cover for their own selfish interests. He cited the fact that workingmen had waived the matter of union recognition when presented with the opportunity to settle with companies for the nine-hour day. Drawing on a variety of sources, Schrembs argued that nine hours of labor produced as many quality goods for industry as ten hours and that it was the manufacturers who continually blocked any peaceful settlement. "We have been trying to correlate a political democracy with industrial feudalism," concluded Schrembs, pointing out the impossible task of bringing democratic popular participation into an arena governed by a small, autocratic group of company owners and managers.[11]

The city's manufacturers responded to Schrembs's charges by claiming that they were unappreciated and abused by the community. In an open letter in the *Furniture Manufacturer and Artisan,* Francis Campau asserted that Schrembs promoted discord by encouraging a sense of ingratitude among the working class for all the benefits that they had reaped through the factory owners' efforts. "The men who are the owners and managers of the furniture factories in this city...lived here all their lives. They and their ancestors are to be credited with making for Grand Rapids the name it has in the world today as a furniture center." It was unjust, he claimed, "to insinuate...they are conducting slave-driving institutions and standing as the oppressors of labor."

Campau reiterated his earlier claim that worker dissatisfaction was the fault of outside agitators. Among these he included the American Federation of Labor as well as Bishop Schrembs and Mayor Ellis, neither of whom had grown up in Grand Rapids, as most of the furniture leaders had, but had come to the city as adults. According to Campau, "There was the best of feeling and good will between the manufacturers and the workers...to the time when their minds were poisoned by the present Mayor, who showed no hesitancy to gain political ends by denouncing" the manufacturers. In this version of events, the workers had been passive and happy working for factory owners who had their best interests at heart, and they became upset only when selfish politicians and community "outsiders" stirred up dissatisfaction.[12]

Ellis's "lies," continued Campau, "are undoubtedly more to blame for the present conditions" than any other factor to be considered. Bishop Schrembs, he said, likewise played a crucial role by hewing to the mayor's agenda on the citizens committee. By Campau's account, the manufacturers pledged themselves to an open shop because that was the only guarantee for the continued success of the furniture business in Grand Rapids. The blessings brought by these businessmen made for nothing but peace and harmony, since "it is a well known fact that the furniture center in the United States boasts of more happy homes and favorable working conditions in life and work for the worker" than anywhere else in the United States.[13]

In Campau's view, the Grand Rapids manufacturers led more honorable lives than their national counterparts because they had sacrificed the chance for higher profits in more advantageous locations in order to build up the industry in Grand Rapids. These leaders "have maintained a system whereby every furniture worker in the city of Grand Rapids was free to sell his labor at the highest price obtainable, without any understandings or agreements on our part, we have carried this spirit into our business." If anybody was guilty of generating baneful influences, it was "the authorities who have refused to show that life and property are safe in this city."[14]

Stories in the city's newspapers provided a different version of events. Assessing the causes contributing to the May 15 riot, the *Evening News* pointed out that Harry Widdicomb's factory sustained damage while the next-door plant managed by his uncle, William Widdicomb, did not. The rioters evidently were careful to distinguish between the two factories, selecting Harry Widdicomb's plant as the target for their anger because he had remained open from the strike's outset, boldly transporting strikebreakers in his automobile. By contrast, William Widdicomb had closed his factory and paid all the loyal workers a partial salary, telling them to stay home and out of harm's way. Harry, not William, had brandished a pistol weeks earlier, generating hostility among the gathered crowds.[15] Provocation came from Harry Widdicomb, and when tempers burst their bounds, workers knew which Widdicomb looked after his workers and which one used his workers to make a point.

A Hardening Stance

Meanwhile, the manufacturers hardened their stance against the workers by bringing in strikebreakers from Pullman, Illinois. The Grand Rapids Show Case Company set up dormitories on its sixth floor — complete with showers and a kitchen staffed by four cooks and several waiters — to house 150 experienced wood workers who had been displaced when the Pullman railroad car company shifted production to passenger cars made of iron and steel. Rumors in the newspapers suggested that the unemployed men from Pullman exceeded 1,000 in number, enough to keep the strike from ever being effective and to produce more than enough goods for the June trade show less than a month away.

Tensions mounted as the trade show deadline approached. The furniture market was the showcase for the city's goods, reflecting and influencing national trends in style, types of wood used, and prices. If the manufacturers could meet the challenge of turning out sufficient furniture with the strike in progress, then disheartened strikers might be more inclined to settle on terms favorable to the industrialists. The strategy did not seem unreasonable. At least one of the strike's early victories faded from view when the first company to accede to worker demands, the Marvel Company, a small manufacturer of rockers and chairs located east of the Grand River near Fairbanks Street and North Avenue, went into receivership as the result of cash flow problems. Despite the fact that the company's assets exceeded its liabilities and that it was expected to emerge from receivership and resume production in a few months, the shutdown lent credibility to the FMA's assertion that unionization bred bankruptcy.[16]

Manufacturers representatives asserted that the June show would take place, no matter what. The show was critical not only for the local industry, but would also serve as a test of solidarity among furniture manufacturers across the country. Even if the Grand Rapids furniture men were unable to fill some of their orders, other manufacturers were expected to avoid taking advantage of their misfortune. Evidence of cooperation at the summer show would demonstrate that local manufacturers' claims to be the frontline "shock troops" against unionization had been taken seriously.

In a series of articles published in national trade journals, Grand Rapids industrialists asserted their blamelessness in the Widdicomb riot, telling fellow employers nationwide that the Polish and Lithuanian workers, who made up the bulk of the factories' "common labor," had been putty in the hands of the city's unscrupulous mayor. They also claimed that Ellis used his political skill to prey upon the 38-firm furniture consortium by adroitly manipulating the city's foreign element, which had been "responsible for most of the demonstrations which have occurred."[17]

The fallout from the May 15 riot continued for several weeks as both the manufacturers and the strikers tried to project favorable images nationwide. The industrialists turned to their trade journals to reach a national audience while the strikers relied on national magazines such as *Outlook*. Edited by former President Theodore Roosevelt and progressive Congregational theologian Lyman Abbott, this journal, sympathetic to the workers' cause, portrayed Grand Rapids' industrialists as backward-looking men, effectively acting as bullies to keep an arbitration process from taking place. In every respect, Abbott's journal mirrored the positions taken by Schrembs and Ellis.

On the local level, Ellis claimed the furniture manufacturers acted through the nominally unbiased civic organization, the Citizens Alliance, to discredit his administration. In an open letter to the city's newspapers on May 22, he described the ongoing confrontation as the "Interests" versus the "People" and charged that the entire source of trouble stemmed from the industrialists' desire to control the city. The mayor also brought up the Brunswick-Balke affair, claiming the furniture men had driven out the large unionized firm because they feared it might compete with them for domination of the city's labor force by paying higher wages. Ellis further stated, "An official never knows what hell really is until he refuses to be the willing tool of the moneyed interests. I appreciate that every person who worships the man with a fat pocketbook, whether a preacher

[Reverend Wishart] or lawyer [Francis Campau] will rally to the support of the manufacturers in some shape. Would it not be in nobler work if the same efforts were used at arbitration and ending the strike which you are making for a military display?"

Ellis's assertion that the factory owners were less concerned about the welfare of the community than they were about retaining an inexpensive pool of skilled labor was put to the test when representatives from the Advertising Club and Industrial Bureau from Buffalo, New York, made overtures to several local firms to relocate to that city, claiming a better labor-management climate. Despite the furor aroused by Buffalo's attempted plunder of the Grand Rapids furniture industry, not much actually happened. Moving would have been enormously expensive, and unionization could be a problem in Buffalo as well as Grand Rapids. In the manufacturers' view, therefore, it would be better to break the union's back in Grand Rapids and do it with the summer furniture show. The Buffalo threat soon faded, and by the end of May the city's newspaper editorials were chastising "poor old Buffalo" for its own failures, blatant opportunism and even the "abject apology" extended by the Buffalo Board of Trade.[18]

Of greater concern to the FMA at this point was the fact that the American Seating Company had settled with its employees. In exchange for a nine-hour workday, the 700-man workforce agreed not to recognize the union and to continue working under the piece-rate system. The FMA's official response denigrated the settlement, saying that American Seating, which served the interests of the Chicago "seating trust," could afford to be generous.[19]

With the critical summer buyers show now less than three weeks away, attention shifted from Buffalo and American Seating to the local district court as the manufacturers pursued litigation to break the unions. Court proceedings for the permanent injunction against the union pickets sought by the FMA opened on May 29 and were scarcely less contentious than the strike itself. When United Brotherhood of Carpenters and Joiners representative William McFarlane entered the courtroom to a round of applause, one of the FMA attorneys derided the enthusiastic reception as the "chorus of a comic opera."[20] Then McGeorge Bundy, chief counsel for the FMA, presented his clients' request for an injunction.

Interestingly, attorney Sybrant Wessalius, who also served as the city's chief legal counsel, represented the strikers in seeking a counter-injunction. If it were not enough that the city's chief legal adviser served as the union's attorney, then the grounds for his counter-injunction offered a further aggravation for the manufacturers. Wessalius asserted that the furniture manufacturers colluded with the Citizens Alliance to crush the union and dominate the city's economy. Furthermore, he charged that they conspired to keep wages artificially low through the use of a blacklist and boycotts.

Continuing to paint the manufacturers in the darkest terms possible, he cited the ouster of the Nachtegall Manufacturing Company from the FMA as an example of punishment for breaking ranks among the manufacturers. Indeed, it had been front-page news only weeks before that the Nachtegall Company president, Albert N. Nachtegall, had been "asked" to resign from the furniture association. Wessalius also pointed out as an example of the FMA's power the fact that the Furniture City Car Loading Company secured favorable freight rates for FMA members to the exclusion of others. Ultimately, for Wessalius, the strike's origins emanated from the "direct result of such conspiracy among the complainants, especially the binding of the industrial manufacturers under pain of losing their membership in the association not to consider any proposition by a committee of their men."

Wessalius maintained that his clients had called the strike over working conditions and the increasing gap between wages and the cost of living. As their income remained steady and prices climbed, workers simply could not afford to pay for life's necessities. Beginning in July 1910, all attempts at dealing with the industry had failed, and it was only after January 1911 that William McFarlane of the United Brotherhood of Carpenters and Joiners came to Grand Rapids, not as an outside agitator, as the industrialists so often argued, but as an adviser invited by the workers. In closing, Wessalius conjured up an image of the manufacturers as the ones in pursuit of violent confrontation, asserting that in the wake of the May 15 riot, William Widdicomb had declared, "Good, now we can get the troops," a reference to calling out the state militia and imposing silence on the strikers at gun point.[21]

Deadlock

In the end, the hearing for a permanent injunction was postponed, although a temporary injunction kept union pickets away from the plant gates. After ten weeks of the strike both sides remained deadlocked. A few independent manufacturers had settled with the strikers, but the total number of reinstated workers represented less than one-quarter of the citywide furniture industry workforce. As the important summer buyers show approached, both sides had drawn blood. But the furniture workers were the worse for it. Support for the strike had peaked, and as the weeks wore on the workmen's ranks dwindled.

Part of the problem was money. The cabinetmakers – the most skilled of the strikers – had enough short-term financial support from their union to keep going. Others were not so lucky. Despite the fact that the United Brotherhood of Carpenters and Joiners had attracted more than 200 new members, an estimated 1,000 men had left the city in search of work. The finishers were in worse shape. By the end of May, their union, predominantly Polish in its membership, faced the continued strike with insufficient funds to provide strike benefits for its rank and file. Membership, which had peaked at 1,400, fell to 500 as men left for work in other cities after their strike benefits ran out. The carpenters union had sent money to help the ailing finishers earlier in the strike, but could not guarantee further assistance.[22]

On the manufacturers' side of the ledger, the Grand Rapids Show Case Company's efforts to import and house strikebreakers earlier in May met with only limited success. Many of the men brought in from Chicago found the living and working conditions intolerable and the absence of fire escapes very troubling. Large quantities of wood shavings and glue inside the factories posed a danger of combustion while angry strikers outside the plants threatened combustion of another sort.

In addition, many of the imported workers were proving ineffective replacements. Newspaper articles reported that many of the substitutes simply drew wood through the machines in order to give the impression of working. Readers got the feeling that if the strikers could just hold out a little longer, then the manufacturers' capitulation was assured. Francis Campau countered by declaring that at least 1,800 workers had returned to their jobs, more than enough to guarantee goods in time for the June show.[23]

Each week, the continuing strike dealt a further blow to the local economy, emphasizing the central role played by the furniture industry. Caught in the middle were the thousands of shopkeepers, merchants and laborers not directly affiliated with the furniture factories, but whose lives depended on the furniture workers' weekly wages that paid the rent, purchased groceries, clothing and other necessities and provided the wherewithal for evenings at the local tavern. The money then circulated from one neighborhood business to another and beyond as grocers, tavern owners and clothiers did business with area distributors, sending those same weekly wages into a cycle of buying and selling that boosted the city's economy.

The *Evening Press* warned in an editorial that the longer the strike continued, the greater the hardship the community endured. Weekly furniture factory payrolls usually exceeded $150,000, according to the newspaper, but now less than a tenth of that total dribbled out. The *Press* urged formation of an arbitration committee to bring peace to the city, noting that unionization and union recognition were not the stumbling blocks that the manufacturers claimed them to be.[24] The city's trade union journal, the *Observer,* stated, "There is good reason to worry about the financial embarrassment of the finishers, but no one need feel concerned about the status of the strike" because even if the finishers returned to work, the cabinetmakers' resistance would carry the day.[25]

As had been feared in March, the fight between factory workers and owners had spilled out to affect the entire community. In some minds, it was the manufacturers' stubbornness that caused the increasing hardships; others began to doubt the strikers' wisdom in walking off the job. In any case, all agreed that the sooner the deadlock ended, the better off the entire city would be. For the manufacturers, control over the union pickets was a key to breaking the strike. There had always been workers who refused to strike, and the FMA reasoned that if union men were kept away from factory gates, the crowds that harassed and intimidated nonstriking workers would disperse, opening the way for more strikers to return to the plants. The court battle for a permanent injunction against the pickets once more assumed center stage.

Their Day in Court

The weekly *Creston News,* which ardently supported the strikers, carried detailed accounts of the manufacturers' efforts to obtain the permanent injunction and the workers' attempts to thwart them. In one report, the paper told its readers that affidavits presented by Sybrant Wessalius demonstrated "pretty conclusively the desire of the manufacturers to bring about violence and martial law in Grand Rapids."[26] Describing sworn statements declaring that some of the city's furniture men "gloated" over the trouble at the Widdicomb factories, the *News* suggested that some of the industrial leaders had helped to provoke the sporadic violence in the Widdicomb factory's neighborhood that erupted into the mid-May riot.

Accounts in daily newspapers, although less biased than those in the *Creston News,* brought home the intensity of the court proceedings. At one point McGeorge Bundy and Mayor George Ellis broke into a brief but heated exchange in which Bundy conceded that the furniture companies were out to crush the unions regardless of any other issues raised. He also charged that the strikers acted in bad faith by walking out before the citizens committee had finished its work, and he railed at the committee for assuming it had powers of arbitration when, in fact, such powers had never been granted.[27]

Judge John S. MacDonald finally announced his decision almost fourteen weeks into the strike and after nearly three weeks of acrimonious testimony. His ruling offered something to both sides: While he prohibited union pickets from standing next to the plants, he did allow strikers to remain in the vicinity of the factories where they could attempt to dissuade returning workers, count the number of men going in, and gauge the amount of work being done. Technically, this was a preliminary decision, not a final pronouncement, which meant that neither party could appeal it to a higher state court.[28] MacDonald had effectively locked a compromise in place for either the duration of the strike or until he issued a final pronouncement on the injunction.

Thwarted in their efforts to secure a permanent injunction, the furniture manufacturers again used their trade journals to take their case to a national business audience. In the pages of the June issue of the monthly *Furniture Manufacturer and Artisan,* for example, they assailed Grand Rapids' daily newspapers as the "most startling exhibition of a partisan and servile press" in the hire of "labor agitators," where everything favorable to the manufacturers' point of view was "belittled, distorted or entirely emasculated." The city's newspapers were governed by "political rather than business or moral influences," said the *Artisan,* and they were examples of poorly run business ventures, animated by deep-seated jealousy of the more successful furniture industrialists.

In making their case against the strikers, the manufacturers talked of an alliance of the "hopelessly ignorant and lawless Poles and Lithuanians" who stopped their carnage and "frenzied defiance of the law, order and authority only long enough to cheer Mayor Ellis." "Truly the mayor and the Poles work well in double harness," exclaimed the *Artisan,* finding it incomprehensible that the community remained sympathetic to the strikers. After all, the journal argued, ordinary people should sympathize with the factory owners who started out "from the bench" or "on the road" and worked their way up the ladder just like anyone else.

The factory owners saw themselves as liberal and public-minded men, proud of their ability to call their workers by name. Sour grapes accounted for the ill will they engendered, fumed the *Artisan,* and local papers sided with the workers simply because the manufacturers did not advertise locally. The FMA's refusal to endorse the annual "industrial edition" of the city's papers represented a rebuff of a "little gentle graft" to keep the favorable images rolling on the front page. As proof of its allegations, the attack concluded, "It was only after the findings of the commission of inquiry that public sentiment began to turn towards the factories."[29]

This presentation of events positioned the manufacturers to appeal for national cooperation from other furniture manufacturers in accommodating shortages bound to appear during the upcoming June buyers show. Not content to let their image be sullied by the newspapers or courtroom invective of Wessalius and Ellis, the manufacturers worked through the Grand Rapids Board of Trade to appoint a three-man committee to examine the charges that the FMA had driven out various competing industries. Since Reverend Wishart headed the committee, it remained unlikely that its work would have much credibility among factory workers.

Ambush

During the first week of June, the strikers called a series of meetings to raise funds and respond to the verbal barrage leveled by the manufacturers. Mayor Ellis sent his secretary, Roman Glocheski, to attend meetings of the finishers and carpenters. A disappointing fund-raiser collected less than $100, and little else of a concrete nature took place save for a protest launched against the *Artisan* article and a resolution to continue with the strike.

Despite the pledge of solidarity, the number of workers returning to their jobs continued to climb. Increasingly, the most diehard strikers began using ambush as a tool to keep wavering workers away from the factories. Those remaining on strike and their supporters watched this intimidation with approval, especially since money was growing scarce and the strikers' endurance was threatened. An especially effective attack took place on June 13 outside the John Widdicomb Company plant with telling results. Workers from the predominantly Polish neighborhood reporting for work were waylaid and forced to turn back by angry strikers. Those who resisted were beaten. On the day before the incident, 100 men had gone through the factory gates; on the day after, fewer than 25 showed up for work.[30]

These attacks did not occur under the cover of darkness. Nor were they perpetrated by crowds of people seeking anonymity in numbers. Instead, they took place in open view as the neighborhood looked on. But fear of the strike enforcers faded as economic necessity compelled growing numbers of men back to the shop floor. Less than a week after the initial attack, more than fifty men came back to their jobs, willing to run the gauntlet of stones that had been set up along the curb in anticipation of their return.

Fractures in the Polish neighborhoods reflected divisions among all strikers. As the rifts became more public, the city's newspapers shifted some of their attention away from the causes of the strike and the manufacturers' charges to matters of religious and ethnic tensions. On June 14, an *Evening Press* editorial explained that there were many motives behind the desire of some workers to return to the plants. Aiming its comments at Poles and Lithuanians, the paper noted that those coming back were not blindly following orders from the industrialists nor committed to breaking the strike. Rather, "many who refused to strike did so because of conscientious scruples. Their religious beliefs on the subject are such as to make them view affiliation with a union" as reluctantly as a Catholic might view consolidation with a Protestant church.

This editorial shift toward sympathy for nonstrikers was a call to understand the cultural differences that made total community cooperation impossible. The *Press* said that ethnic and religious differences could not be expected to vanish in the face of economic issues. For many, said a June 15 *Press* editorial, a man's relation to his God and his conscience took precedence over his class interests. This editorial, coupled with the ongoing investigation of the union by the Christian Reformed Church, portended an ever-declining strength among the strikers.

Undercurrents of economic need, along with class and cultural differences, lay just below the surface of solidarity when 3,000 strikers and their families attended a picnic at John Ball Park on the city's west side. Samuel Gompers, president of the American Federation of Labor, was scheduled to speak, but cancelled his appearance. His initial commitment, however, suggested that the Grand Rapids strike had assumed more than a little importance for the national labor movement. Speeches given by McFarlane, Ellis, and Wessalius received cheers from the crowd.

Meanwhile, factory owners continued their efforts to offset the power wielded on behalf of the strikers by Mayor Ellis. In the face of what they perceived as sympathy for the strikers on the part of city police, and inaction by the state militia, manufacturers turned to Kent County Sheriff William J. Hurley to build an auxiliary army as a response to the mayor's peace patrols. Hurley responded swiftly by deputizing strikebreakers and nonstriking employees loyal to the factory owners.[31] Tensions between the city and county forces grew amid rumors that the newly deputized workers might carry firearms, setting the stage for a serious confrontation between city and county authorities.

Peaceful Resistance

As the buyers show approached, strikers saw it more and more as the make-or-break moment for their cause. If they could keep new products from coming to market, they reasoned, company owners would have to admit the strike was effective, and pressure for meaningful negotiations would build. On the other hand, a successful show would demonstrate the ineffectiveness of the strike and lead to more workers returning to their jobs. The strikers welcomed any demonstration of support. It was at least a moral victory, for example, when furniture workers in nearby Holland recognized the style being sent through their line as something quite different from their own company's goods. They refused to do the work, saying, "This is not our line and we will not get it out, for we believe that is for a Grand Rapids factory."[32]

Economic support for the strikers trickled in slowly. The beleaguered finishers union happily accepted $500 raised by a citywide collection effort and a benefit ball sponsored by the Holland-American Aid Society. But the amount was small compared to the weekly benefits needed by the nearly 3,000 workers still on strike. It was beginning to look as though the strike would collapse if the summer show succeeded.[33]

Determined to endure through the summer, striking workers from two of the largest FMA plants, Berkey & Gay and Sligh, returned to their respective factories to retrieve their tools. In a day when skilled tradesmen owned their own tools rather than rely upon the employer to provide them, leaving behind these valuable personal assets symbolized the workers' faith that they would eventually return to their jobs on their own terms. Left on their workbenches, the tools also denoted the sense of trust between workers and factory owners that had existed at the beginning of the walkout. When the workers took their tools away, they further widened the breach between strikers and owners.

Over three days in mid-June, scores of workers marched into the factories and picked up their tools, signaling their commitment to continue the strike even though support seemed to be wavering. Despite other currents pushing workers into conflict with one another, here was a seemingly spontaneous effort at solidarity by a significant number of workers. In several factories workers debated among themselves about taking such a dramatic step. It would not be easy. Many of the men retrieving their tools had worked for twenty years or more in a single shop; they found it hard to "wrench themselves loose from all the old associations without more than a passing thought of the seriousness of their act." Employees at the Widdicomb Company, Oriel, Grand Rapids Chair, Nelson-Matter, and Raab Chair all debated taking the dramatic step, and many followed through.[34]

Expanding their message through peaceful, determined resistance, several hundred workers paraded through the West Side factory district, but deliberately avoided the violence-prone John Widdicomb factory. The workers' action brought a howl of indignation from McGeorge Bundy who called for parade leaders to be jailed, claiming, "The parade, so called, was the most flagrant violation of the injunction imaginable," and took place only to intimidate workers returning to their jobs. "If there is anything which the court's injunction forbids, it is just this and we promise to punish, if possible, the men who took part in this demonstration." Judge MacDonald (recognizing the workers right to peaceful demonstrations) refused to jail the marchers.[35]

The self-imposed discipline among the central core of workers and their pursuit of a common goal belied the manufacturers' claims that most workers were "lawless and ignorant."

High-Handed Tactics

To the extent the strikers had pinned their hopes for victory on a failed summer buyers show, they were doomed to disappointment. Despite a slow start, a national economic slowdown, and an overall decline in the volume of orders, Grand Rapids' summer 1911 furniture show, which opened on June 26 and ran through July 22, picked up considerable attendance by the end of its nearly month-long run. Cooperative buyers generally made fewer-than-expected demands on the Grand Rapids producers. Many of the 954 registered buyers agreed to accept delays in new items, purchase older styles and take delivery from inventories of existing stock. Although production in Grand Rapids factories lagged seriously behind capacity, for the most part, competing manufacturers did not try to take work away from Grand Rapids. The industry-wide fear that a workers' victory might introduce "disruptive influences" into other plants helped to make the show a success. The Grand Rapids FMA pledged to hold firm against the strikers, even if it took until "August, 1912!" The furniture men declared they would never budge. "Every man should understand that proposition first, last and all the time."[36]

The manufacturers meant what they said. In early July a group of strikers stood on the Union Depot platform in Grand Rapids watching a trainload of strikebreakers from Philadelphia and Chicago pull into the station. A "near riot" erupted after Sheriff Hurley tossed one of the watching strikers onto the tracks.[37] When the Philadelphia men learned they had walked into an ongoing strike, not a "labor shortage" as the manufacturers' recruiter had told them, they claimed they had been brought to the city under false pretenses and sought compensation and train fare back to Philadelphia. Ultimately a Grand Rapids court awarded them $29 each to help defray the cost of the trip home.[38] In another incident, the city physician stopped more than a dozen smallpox-infected strikebreakers from coming into the city. Rumors circulated that nearly twenty had already slipped into town.[39]

In response to the FMA's tactics, popular opinion strengthened in support of the strikers. From their Indianapolis headquarters, the national carpenters union sent more than $100,000, raised in part through a 50-cent levy on each union member in the country, to replenish the depleted strike benefit fund. The timely appearance of the money was a gratifying show of support that helped both the carpenters and finishers see their way through several weeks more without wages.

On July 15 a massive parade of 3,000 strikers, organized with the permission of Mayor Ellis, marched through the city's main streets displaying banners that echoed their financial needs. With good humor some of the signs expressed hope that there would be "no prospect of eating snowballs in the winter" even though the "manufacturers wish-hart for us to give in." One banner asked whether or not Grand Rapids would "always be ruled by the Manufacturers' Association" and carried the rejoinder: "Who Made Grand Rapids Famous?" The parade culminated in a gathering of the marchers and their sympathizers in Fulton Street Park (now Veterans Park) where Wessalius, Ellis, and an organizer from the American Federation of Labor lauded the strikers' efforts and praised their restraint in the face of provocation.[40]

The day of the parade, the *Evening Press* reprinted an editorial from *Outlook,* Theodore Roosevelt's publication. The former president came down hard against the industrialists and praised both the strikers and Mayor Ellis's innovative use of the peace patrols. "It seems to us," wrote Roosevelt, "that the strikers not only had a perfect right to be special policemen, but that they are deserving of commendation for acting as police until they show by some sort of over-action that they are unworthy of confidence. There is no more reason for declaring that a striker is out of place as a policeman than for saying that the son of a capitalist is out of place as a member of the militia."[41]

The *Evening News* followed up with its own editorial that defended the "manly deportment of the strikers" who had the courage to "stand in defense of a principle" while shaming the manufacturers for prolonging the strike through stubborn intransigence. Not only did the industrialists visit disruption on the community by refusing to consider reasonable worker requests, said the *News,* but they further damaged the integrity of the city by bringing in "strangers" of unknown character to keep the factories going. The city that prided itself on family life, churchly values, and a high rate of home ownership found an influx of unknown men at its doorsteps, outsiders coming to perform the unwelcome task of breaking the strike. Would these newcomers have the same sense of community loyalty, the paper asked rhetorically, that local workers shared?[42]

Settlement with the Fancy Furniture Company came the same week in mid-July as the parade and the strong editorials. Fancy had been one of the firms whose workers returned briefly in order to remove their tools, and this symbolic action may have influenced its president, David Uhl, to break ranks with the other manufacturers. In any event, Uhl announced negotiations that secured increased pay and shorter hours for his employees without invoking union recognition. Helping to confirm public perceptions that the FMA was largely to blame for the strike's impact on the local economy and its disruption of public life was his comment that "not being a member of the employers' association I am at perfect liberty to use my own judgment in making any settlements that I might desire."[43]

By the end of July, the city council acted in behalf of the strikers by passing a resolution that banned the importation of strikebreakers. Echoing the words of the *Evening News,* the resolution's language, although it lacked the force of law, expressed fear of community disruption by outside influences and stated that the importation of strikebreakers "cannot but have a serious effect upon the social conditions in the city" by bringing unemployment to known men of quality and replacing them with "men of questionable character." Such unwelcome residents "being thrown onto their own resources" would become a threat to the city's "peace and safety."

The *Evening News* joined in the condemnation, lambasting the manufacturers for their "public be damned" attitude and reporting that "there is growing day by day among the citizens of Grand Rapids, a feeling that this kind of indifference [by the manufacturers] has crept into the local industrial situation. The thought is rapidly gaining ground that Grand Rapids can ill afford to remain subjected to an industry which can be so conducted or manipulated that the welfare of the whole city may be crippled." Set against this background, news that the finishers union had received gifts totaling $2,500 was a statement of solidarity against the influence exercised by the furniture manufacturers.[44]

But popular sentiment alone would not carry the day. The strikers had to find a way to bring the manufacturers to the negotiating table. But the furniture men's superior economic resources coupled with a successful summer trade show permitted them to play for time.

The Beginning of the End

Time and money seemed to be on the side of the manufacturers. The United Brotherhood of Carpenters and Joiners organizer McFarlane left town on August 1 to observe the massive labor convulsions shaking Great Britain after rail and shipyard workers had shut down all traffic. In his farewell speech to the Grand Rapids strikers, he praised their admirable restraint in the face of provocation, saying that he had "seen more trouble at a wedding in East Buffalo than has occurred in all of this fight." Voicing confidence in ultimate victory, McFarlane nonetheless raised the possibility of defeat. "When you ask next time to sit down for a conference they will listen to you," he assured the crowd, promising continued support even after he had gone. After all, "Do you suppose the organization has spent $127,000 here and is putting in $8,000 a week knowing that you can't win? I think you have a fine A-1 chance to win this fight."[45]

At first it seemed there might still be hope for a settlement. Newspapers reported that the Gunn Company – an FMA member – had offered favorable terms to its 300 workers. If it were true, this would have been the largest settlement since the American Seating Company returned to production in May, and the first time an FMA firm had come to terms with its workforce. However, FMA secretary Francis Campau cautioned newsmen to "be careful" about their stories to the public. "I understand," warned Campau, "that the men go back…on just the terms which existed when the strike began." Unfortunately for the strikers, Campau was right. J. P. Homillier, manager of the Gunn factory, denied that any settlement had taken place, further stating, "Before we will submit to union combination we will close our factory."[46]

On August 9, the same day that Gunn refuted newspaper accounts of settlement with the strikers, the Christian Reformed Church's classis announced its findings on union membership. In a far-reaching report that affected nearly one-third of the remaining strikers, church leaders announced that membership in the carpenters union was incompatible with church membership. The union was "not based on the brotherhood of man, but it is for material purposes only," read the key charge, with additional harsh words for the burial rites practiced by members of the United Brotherhood of Carpenters and Joiners.

According to the classis, which represented seventeen churches and 8,000 congregants, it was the union's preoccupation with material – rather than spiritual – concerns that most offended the church. The union's principles stood anchored "merely" in "principles of humanity and earthly welfare without recognizing God in any respect." The union sought only "human good" and "no more." Instead of joining unions, church members should turn to their pastors who should, in turn, "attempt to touch more often on economic and social affairs in their sermons." The FMA eagerly offered to reprint and circulate the decision, but officials of the classis declined.[47]

The Collapse

As the men of the Christian Reformed Church began returning to work, remaining diehard strikers received another bitter pill when word came that the United Brotherhood of Carpenters and Joiners would no longer provide benefits to those who remained out. At an August 18 meeting attended by an estimated 2,000 workers, the men voted three to one in favor of going back under the old conditions.

In the end, the strikers' return to work was more than a repudiation of the concept of shared control of the workplace; the defeat also greatly diminished union activity in Grand Rapids. The local groups associated with the United Brotherhood of Carpenters and Joiners lost over 50 percent of their membership. Although the American Federation of Labor remained active in Grand Rapids, it too was weakened and, for the most part, turned its interest to other locations and other industries that offered greater potential for success.

Remarkably, after all that had been said during the heat of the strike, the FMA did not gloat over its victory. Instead of recriminations, it offered only regrets that many fine men had been "misled by their leaders." These sentiments, voiced by Robert Irwin and echoed by others, were a clear expression of a paternalistic view of the strikers as errant wards of the industrialists rather than as determined men who had taken a calculated risk to better their situation. Instead of seeing the organized workers as equals, furniture manufacturers looked upon the workforce as a resource that, if managed prudently, would benefit employer and worker alike. It was that attitude that led the manufacturers to create their own banks, production groups, and shipping pools. The view also gave rise to Employers Association efforts to track the movement and wages of each workingman in the industry while keeping government intervention at arm's length.

Now, factory owners wanted a return to the status quo as quickly as possible. One unidentified factory owner said, "Now is the time for all parties concerned to buckle down and do their best for the city and its chief industry. The sooner the recent trouble is forgotten, the better."[48] The Berkey & Gay Company's treasurer, George G. Whitworth, made similar remarks to the press. "I am sure I voice the sentiments of all manufacturers when I say that we have only the kindliest feeling for our men. You may say that we shall do our part to take care of all of them at the very earliest possible moment. There may not be work for all of our old men at first, but as soon as it is possible we hope to have them all back in the shops."

The *Evening News* criticized this condescending attitude, noting that such an outlook could not long continue. The strike's causes were not merely economic in origin, said the *News,* but "a local manifestation of world wide unrest under present industrial conditions." A partnership in production to assure fair treatment and a sense of social democracy was essential under the new conditions of modern life, argued the paper, but "this cannot be done by denying to the workers their inherent rights, nor by treatment that in any way evidences the autocrat."[49]

The FMA members did not share this vision. They blamed the strike's duration and widespread support on government leaders who pandered to its participants when they should have taken a hard line. City government's role under the leadership of Mayor George Ellis so infuriated the furniture manufacturers that their leaders began to work with key members of the city's Board of Trade to model a reform effort aimed at replacing the current form of government with something much more to their liking.

Beginning in 1912, in the aftermath of the strike, they mounted a municipal reform movement aimed at creating a government that effectively concentrated power in the hands of business leaders while diluting the influence of the ordinary voter. Taking aim at the city's unruly west side and the influence exercised by a popular mayor, they proposed a new city charter that would remake the city in the image of a privately held corporation where a small board of directors governed affairs by setting policy and hiring professional management.

Endnotes

1. Grand Rapids' daily newspapers all provided front-page coverage of the West Side riot. This account relied on the *Evening News,* May 16, 1911, pp. 1-2; and the *Press,* May 16, 1911, p. 1.
2. *Press,* May 16, 1911, p. 1.
3. Ibid.
4. Ibid. p. 10; *Evening News,* May 17, 1911, p. 1.
5. *Press,* May 19, 1911, p. 7.
6. *Evening News,* May 16, 1911, p. 1; May 17, 1911, p. 1.
7. *Outlook,* June 17, 1911, p. 326.
8. Both Bundy and Campau were associated with prominent families. Campau was the grandson of Antoine Campau, brother of Grand Rapids founder, Louis Campau. Bundy's son, also named McGeorge Bundy, served as national security adviser to both President John F. Kennedy and President Lyndon B. Johnson.
9. *Evening News,* May 17, 1911, p. 1.
10. *Press,* May 17, 1911, pp. 1, 14.
11. *Evening News,* May 18, 1911, p. 9.
12. *Furniture Manufacturer and Artisan,* June 1911, pp. 211-15.
13. *Evening News,* May 19, 1911, pp. 1-2.
14. *Furniture Manufacturer and Artisan,* loc.cit.
15. *Evening News,* May 19, 1911, pp. 1-2.
16. Ibid. May 20, 1911, p. 1.
17. Ibid. May 24, 1911, pp. 1-2.
18. Ibid. May 22, 1911, p. 1; May 25, 1911, p. 1; May 27, 1911, p. 1; May 29, 1911, p. 1; *Press,* May 26, 1911, p. 6.
19. *Press,* May 26, 1911, p. 1.
20. *Evening News,* May 29, 1911, p. 1.
21. *Press,* May 29, 1911, p. 6.
22. Ibid. May 30, 1911, p. 2; May 31, 1911, p. 1.
23. *Evening News,* June 2, 1911, p. 8.
24. *Press,* June 2, 1911, p. 6.
25. *Observer,* June 5, 1911, p. 2.
26. *Creston News,* June 2, 1911, p. 2.
27. *Evening News,* June 3, 1911, p. 1; *Press,* June 3, 1911, p. 1.
28. Ibid. June 7, 1911, p. 2.
29. *Furniture Manufacturer and Artisan,* June 1911, pp. 211-15.
30. *Press,* June 8, 1911, p. 12; June 11, 1911, p. 2; June 13, 1911, p. 12; *Evening News,* June 13, 1911, p. 3.
31. *Press,* June 14, 1911, p. 9; June 15, 1911, p. 6; June 16, 1911, p. 1; *Evening News,* June 16, 1911, p. 1.
32. *Outlook,* June 17, 1911, p. 326.
33. *Evening News,* June 18, 1911, p. 1.
34. *Observer,* June 19, 1911, p. 1.

35. *Evening News,* June 20, 1911, p. 1; June 27, 1911, p. 1.
36. *Grand Rapids Herald,* June 26, 1911, p. 3; July 22, 1911, p. 3; *Observer,* July 3, 1911, p. 1.
37. *Press,* July 7, 1911, p. 9; *Evening News,* July 7, 1911, p. 1; July 8, 1911, p. 1.
38. *Evening News,* July 12, 1911, p. 1.
39. Ibid. July 25, 1911, p. 1; July 26, p. 1; July 27, 1911, p. 1.
40. Ibid. July 15, p. 1; *Press,* July 15, 1911, p. 4.
41. *Outlook,* July 15, 1911, p. 566.
42. *Evening News,* July 17, 1911, p. 6.
43. Ibid. July 22, 1911, p. 1; *Press,* July 21, 1911, p. 1.
44. *Observer,* July 31, 1911, p. 1.
45. *Evening News,* August 1, 1911, p. 10.
46. *Press,* August 8, 1911, p. 1; August 9, 1911, p. 1.
47. *Evening News,* August 9, 1911, p. 6.
48. *Press,* August 18, 1911, p. 1; August 19, 1911. p. 9.
49. *Evening News,* August 19, 1911, p. 1.

Chapter 6

*A Lesser Democracy: Businessmen,
Bankers, and Reform Government 1912 - 1916*

After a long, contentious summer, the end of the furniture strike of 1911 left the city sorely divided. On the political front, the furniture manufacturers viewed Mayor Ellis as an opportunistic politician who supported the workers because he wanted their votes. "He became the chief speaker at most of the gatherings of the men on strike," contended the FMA, charging he never missed the chance to vilify the factory owners and "array capital against labor."[1] Angry with the mayor for his refusal to call in the militia and his use of the worker peace patrols instead, the manufacturers were no less bitter towards the city's aldermen and their unanimous resolution condemning the importation of strikebreakers. The strike had been a "hard fought controversy of great bitterness," according to the industrialists, in which workers had been "misled by the labor leaders and the politicians."[2]

The mayor's supporters responded that he was a legitimate spokesman for the wage earners' interests in a contest of two unequal parties. In this view, it was management that distorted the facts while government behaved properly in its efforts to preserve the peace. Pursuing a negotiated settlement, according to the pro-Ellis faction, served the combined interests of owners, strikers, and the citizens of Grand Rapids, who had all suffered during the strike.

The Political Initiative

Their inability to control city government increased the manufacturers' sense that they had been fortunate to defeat the strikers, and they were aware that success had emerged from factors other than their own strength. For one thing, they had been unable to keep several employers from settling with their striking employees. They also understood that a downturn in the national economy had worked to their advantage, depressing consumer demand for new furniture and enabling their inventory to last longer, thereby reducing the impact of lost production during the walkout. The furniture men remained thankful that Ellis had been unable to intervene directly and impose compulsory arbitration, a step they feared would be an implicit recognition of workers' rights to organize, state their grievances, and bargain collectively. The manufacturers' economic power had played a key role in defeating the 1911 strike, but the mayor's actions throughout left little doubt that political control of city hall held the key to long-term success.

The solution business leaders hit upon was an overhaul of the city charter, which had happened numerous times since the adoption of the original charter in 1850. At the time of the furniture strike, 24 aldermen elected from 12 wards controlled the city's budget, while various appointed boards – including the boards of Police and Fire Commissioners, Public Works, Health, and (Tax) Review and Equalization – and their ward supervisors determined how purchases were made and contracts let. Through their control of the city's purse strings and their ability to distribute patronage appointments, the aldermen and the boards had amassed a great deal of power. After watching city government side with the strikers, business leaders and other conservative members of the community proposed to shift that power into the hands of professional administrators.

The first effort to diffuse the power of the aldermen, ward supervisors, and municipal board members came in early 1910 with the establishment of a charter reform committee headed by furniture manufacturer Robert Irwin, a man of substantial influence on the Grand Rapids Board of Trade and in the local banking industry. Seeking limited reform that would create a stronger administration, Irwin's committee proposed charter revisions that would enhance the mayor's power of appointment and consolidated miscellaneous services under existing departments such as the fire and police boards.[3]

Every newspaper, every business group, and even Mayor Ellis endorsed the reform, but each did so for different reasons. As far as the business community was concerned, consolidating power in the mayor's hands would permit Ellis no excuse for failure. The business leaders believed it would be hard for Ellis to conceal political bargaining or irregularities in government spending and therefore easier to discredit him in the next election. For his part, Ellis wanted to enhance the power of the mayor and to ensure that major services fell into clearly defined departmental jurisdictions after decades of improvisation prompted by rapid growth. The proposed charter revision was enough of a departure to arouse suspicion among the populace, but the changes it offered were not sufficient to excite widespread support. Despite the *Herald's* plea that "all is virtue in pro-charter arguments," voters turned down the proposal in February 1912 by a margin of more than a 10 percent.[4]

It is likely that the furniture strike played a role in the rejection of the charter proposal. The strongest opposition to the charter revisions came from areas dominated by Dutch and Polish populations, areas that had been hardest hit by both the strike and the West Side riot. The greatest support for the proposal came from the hilltop and nearby Second, Third, and Tenth wards, home to bankers, lawyers, and factory owners and managers. Some additional support came from the Eleventh Ward, home to many middle-class professionals, salesmen, and small businessmen. However, the limited numbers in these wards were not sufficient to carry the election.

The majority of voters seemed unwilling to place additional power in the hands of the mayor, preferring a strong city council that paid close attention to local ward-based interests. George Ellis misjudged the extent of opposition to the proposed change and, when the vote failed, expressed disappointment, but carefully avoided further comment. His unusually circumspect behavior was easily explained; he was in the midst of a close campaign for reelection, and with the vote barely a month away, he could ill afford to alienate his core constituency.

A Three-Way Race

The 1912 charter election lacked the intensity of the mayoral race that followed. Ever aware of the power of political symbols, Ellis launched his campaign for a fourth term at the Lincoln Club on February 22, George Washington's birthday.[5] Immediately after his announcement, the Good Government League, which had supported charter reform but opposed Ellis, reissued some of its earlier pamphlets alleging Ellis's personal moral corruption.[6]

Ellis found himself running against two challengers in 1912: George Perry, a Democrat who had served as mayor from 1898 to 1902, and Edward Kosten, a Socialist. In the spirited three-way race that ensued, Perry defined the issues of the election and eventually made decisive inroads into Ellis's traditional area of support on the West Side. To a lesser extent, so did Kosten. Perry charged that Ellis was no friend of the workingman and argued that he offered only symbolic support during the furniture workers strike. The mayor, of course, denied the charge and noted that, as a friend of labor, he had acted during his tenure to restore pension benefits to injured police and fire fighters and to the widows of those killed in the line of duty.

Perry also asserted that Ellis had deliberately limited the number of saloons in the city, a charge that was not without merit. The abstemious "Deacon" Ellis was indeed more of a bluenose than his rhetoric suggested; his record showed that he had worked quietly with the city council to reduce the number of saloons and shorten their operating hours. The number of drinking establishments had dropped from 193 in 1910 to 160 two years later, and the ratio of saloons to citizens had gone from 1:600 to 1:800. In this instance, George Ellis managed to serve the agenda of East Side reformers while giving lip service to the desires of his West Side supporters.[7]

Perry's attack strategy worked well in those precincts with the heaviest concentration of saloons. Ironically, Ellis's newly revealed record of moderation on the ever-volatile saloon issue, plus the success with which he had kept down violence during the furniture strike, allowed him to present himself as the defender of private property. In addition to his traditional support from areas such as the Dutch immigrant community along Grandville Avenue in the Twelfth Ward, he now found strength among his former opponents in the Second, Third, and Tenth wards. However much the Good Government League or the industrialists in their trade journals might have blustered against Ellis, when faced with the prospect of Perry or a Socialist in the mayor's chair, they stood behind a predictable if unloved candidate. When all 14,772 votes were counted, Ellis defeated Perry by 541 votes, 6,499 to 5,958, with Kosten, the Socialist candidate, tallying a surprising 2,315. Combined, Perry's and Kosten's totals denied Ellis a majority, but Kosten gained votes at the expense of Perry, thus leaving Ellis with a decisive plurality and two more years in the mayor's seat.[8]

Perhaps as worrisome to the business community as Ellis's victory was Edward Kosten's more than 2,000 votes, a four-fold increase from the 500 votes garnered by the Socialist candidate in the 1910 mayoral election. Kosten's platform, virtually unchanged from previous Socialist pledges, lacked any direct reference to the strike and promised public ownership of the city's utilities by the workingman, a redistribution of wealth, and a host of general industrial reforms.[9]

His greatest support came in the northeastern quarter of the city and from a sliver of the riverside precincts on the Northwest Side. The North Side's enthusiasm for him appeared to be based on the common ground of class interest.[10] Not discernibly of any single ethnic or religious composition, Kosten's supporters were an amalgam of native-born Protestants bound together by their working-class status.[11] Diverse in employment, they were wage earners who lived in neighborhoods of owner-occupied homes in the middle to lower-third range of value.[12]

Perhaps a key to understanding the Socialist vote rests on the slow rate of economic growth experienced in this part of the city. An area of blue-collar homeowners, the Northeast Side had been bypassed by industrial and residential development. Subdivision developments and property sales ran behind the city's newly annexed Southeast Side; even the fringe areas of the West Side developed more quickly than the northern neighborhoods.[13] Here was a "forgotten" quarter of the city, not bound by ethnic or religious ties, expressing a range of frustrations at the ballot box.

The Winds of Change

Political dissent in Grand Rapids following the furniture strike was not limited to the strong Socialist showing in the mayoral campaign. The presidential election in November 1912 heralded additional winds of change. Normally a Republican stronghold in a Republican state, Grand Rapids returned a strong vote for Democratic nominee Woodrow Wilson. This vote was concentrated in the West

Side precincts that had gone heavily for Democratic Party candidate George Perry in the 1912 mayoral election. Residents of the Seventh, Eighth, and Ninth wards had begun to abandon the Republican Party and Ellis whom they had supported since 1906.

The 1912 elections, both mayoral and presidential, were the first extensive test of the city's political mood following the 1911 strike and suggested several important trends to would-be leaders and reformers. To George Ellis, the ethnic, working-class voters he had courted so intensely sent a message of independence, repudiating his endorsed charter reform. Even with his longstanding reputation as a friend of the wage earner, his alliance with the West Side voters needed to be rebuilt. His stand on the saloon issue had touched a raw nerve among his traditional supporters, who may also have felt uneasy about the additional power the failed charter revision might have given him. The fact that Ellis campaigned for the Bull Moose Party candidate, Theodore Roosevelt, while West Side voters went for Wilson could be read as a signal to Ellis not to take their support for granted.

For members of the reform constituency, lessons came just as plainly. The proposed charter revisions of 1912 had been an effort at compromise and moderation that ended up not pleasing enough voters to pass. Had they been adopted, the revisions would have strengthened the mayor's hand while leaving the old aldermanic system, with its focus on ward politics and patronage, intact. Without the creation of a centralized administrative board, the city's many neighborhoods would still have a major voice in the city's political process through their aldermen. Of even greater concern to the reformers was the possibility that the mayoral position could fall into the hands of someone more extreme than Ellis, someone who might open the city to greater influence from labor leaders and saloon owners.

At the heart of the governmental control issue lay the power to tax, to disburse funds, to regulate public transportation and utilities, and to award liquor licenses and other permits that fell within the city's corporate bounds. Finding jobs for friends, rewarding political donors and supporters, helping ward representatives iron out problems, or securing aid for dislocated and distressed families all fell to the personal prerogatives of the mayor. With Ellis occupying the office, the mayor was a chief executive who held together the contentious factions of workers and employers, immigrants and natives, rich and poor, and a growing middle class. He oversaw the horse-trading that was part and parcel of the local political scene and kept his finger on the pulse of voters' moods by visiting fraternal halls, houses of worship, barbershops, taverns, and other neighborhood gathering places.

As the East Side industrialists and businessmen grew more determined to refashion city government, they sought to change the structure of municipal administration. Admirers of the highly centralized decision-making process of modern corporations, they saw the ideal city government as a corporate hierarchy in which elected commissioners functioned much like a board of directors, setting policies to be executed by expert managers instead of vote-oriented politicians.

Frank M. Sparks, political correspondent for the *Grand Rapids Herald,* advanced the case for reform in a book titled *The Business of Government Municipal Reform,* in which he emphasized parallels between developments in business and government. He wrote that just as ownership in the modern corporation had been divorced from management, so, too, must the individual citizen let professionals guide the direction of municipal life. In the modern business corporation, he argued, stockholders voted on general issues, leaving major policy decisions to boards of directors, who in turn hired chief administrators responsible for the enterprise's day-to-day operation. Citizens, said Sparks, were like shareholders in the modern municipal corporation. If they wanted more efficient government, they must be prepared to surrender direct control of policy to elected commissioners who would serve as a board of directors and, in turn, hire professional managers.[14]

Taking their cue from Sparks, what the industrialists wanted was a change in the basic rules of the game. Rather than alter the form of municipal government in a superficial way, their aim was to do away with the existing system altogether. Instead of electing two aldermen from each of the city's twelve wards to represent voter interests on the city council, the reformers advocated a shift to three wards with a seven-member city commission elected at large. Two city commissioners would represent each ward, and the seventh commissioner, the mayor, who was "first among equals," would preside over the commission. The plan was designed to create a government less responsive to direct citizen participation and the interest groups that dominated specific areas of the city.[15]

Aimed at diluting bloc voting among the community's ethnic constituencies, religious interests, and neighborhood groups, the nonpartisan at-large election of city commissioners would turn the city into a single political unit. By reducing the number of men serving on the council and having those men represent the city at large, hilltop leaders could use their money and organizational skills to elect a council more sympathetic to their point of view. After several missteps and failed attempts at compromise, the business community now had a clear blueprint for changing city government. Several more years would pass, however, before any plan for a new municipal government structure would be put into action.

A New Charter Commission

Economic hardship returned to Grand Rapids with the recession of 1913-14. As part of an unofficial relief program to help increasing numbers of unemployed workers, Mayor Ellis used the city's resources to create jobs.[16] He did this through inter-fund borrowing, taking unused portions of one departmental budget and disbursing the funds elsewhere, notably to parks and street repair, to provide employment for the needy and indigent.[17] While such procedures anticipated strategies later adopted by state and federal governments during the Great Depression, many contemporary critics viewed them as irresponsible.[18] Local newspapers wanted to know why city treasurer George P. Tilma and Mayor Ellis did not agree on the financial health of the city treasury, and furniture manufacturers and other businessmen demanded greater accountability from city officials who controlled budgets.[19]

Toward the end of 1914, the Grand Rapids Association of Commerce (until 1911 known as the Board of Trade) launched an investigation of various city departments in response to charges of waste, mismanagement, and inefficiency.[20] Spearheading this campaign was the Reverend Alfred Wishart, whose long-standing service to the Board of Trade made him a valuable asset to the manufacturers. Although the city would eventually adopt many of the Wishart committee's recommendations, the association's board of directors decided that "piecemeal revision" was not a solution. In January 1915 they announced that extensive charter reform was necessary and called for the creation of a new charter commission.[21]

Mayor Ellis and a majority of the city's aldermen agreed, and a special election gave voters the opportunity to select what would be a 15-member charter commission, with one member elected by each of the city's twelve wards and three more chosen at large. The role of the city's economic leaders in the election was more subtle than it had been on the 1912 charter commission, but no less evident in its influence, for even the working-class Fifth and Fourth wards chose conservative professionals who represented class rather than neighborhood interests – attorney William J. Landman, secretary of the Michigan State Bar Association and member of the 1912 charter commission, and Claude O. Taylor, who owned the Taylor Printing and Publishing Company, one of the first unionized shops in the city. Also chosen by their respective wards were Charles Sligh, Jacob Steketee, and Oscar Kilstrom. Henry Jewell, George Perry, and W. Millard Palmer were elected at large.

Perry and Palmer were former mayors of Grand Rapids and long-time opponents of George Ellis. Sligh, Steketee, and Jewell were hilltop residents and active members of the Association of Commerce; Sligh was a furniture manufacturer, Steketee was a retail merchant, and Jewell was on the Bench.[22] William Oltman, from the Sixth Ward, owned the Oltman Shoe Company. He and Oscar Kilstrom both served on the Association of Commerce and, along with Jewell, worked on the association's committees for municipal and legislative reform. These seven men would consistently line up together against any changes proposed by West Side representatives.

Focusing its efforts on reforming the city government in order to place businessmen in control, the charter commission, began its work in April. Although a host of variations came under consideration, ranging from a manager-mayor system with additional aldermen to a plan for fewer alderman and elimination of the mayor, George Perry's proposal guided the next ten months of debate. Perry suggested the "elimination of ward lines, the abolishing of the office of mayor, aldermen and all appointive boards, and substituting therefore the division of the city into three districts."

Although originally tabled, Perry's radical suggestion returned to dominate discussions by the beginning of June when attorney Edward A. Maher urged commission members to consider a version of the so-called Dayton plan. Like Perry's proposal, the Dayton plan called for a commission-manager form of government composed of at least three and not more than five council members, elected at large, who would serve as both the city's administrative and legislative bodies, and an appointed manager rather than an elected mayor to be chief executive. "I believe that the election of commissioners by the city at large would tend to broader views regarding the municipal welfare and progress," Maher said, "than would their selection from different districts or sections within the city." In plain English, the hilltop reformers were determined to find a way to strip the West Side voters of the strength that the current ward system gave them.

Maher had voiced the most frequently cited criticism of the mayoral system: Dominance of local ward issues sorely inhibited "effective" government, at least as defined by the business leaders. In their view, a strong, centralized authority with the power to treat problems affecting the entire city and allocate resources and services with an eye towards the broader picture would eliminate the petty squabbles that consumed aldermen's time. Commissioners elected at large, argued Maher, would have "a sense of responsibility" that "would be more definite with regard to matters affecting both the general and local interests of the city." What Maher did not say was that the at-large election of city commissioners would take away from the Poles and other immigrant groups the power to bargain effectively with the city leadership through their aldermen.

The East Side reformers on the charter commission next addressed the issue of the mayor. Commission members wanted to know if a mayor was legally required at all and, if so, must he be popularly elected? Not necessarily, said the commission's judiciary subcommittee. Based on its interpretation of Michigan's Home Rule Act, the subcommittee affirmed that a mayor was required by law, but suggested that any new municipal charter could provide for his election "either by a direct vote of the people or by a body of representatives chosen by the people."

Electing the mayor by a "body of representatives chosen by the people" opened the door to a commission form of government. Once authority had been vested in a commission elected by the voters at large, that body could act in the name of the people to choose a mayor. Satisfied of the legality in removing the mayor from popular election, the reform commission then moved on to deal with the job of city manager, who would have "all power and responsibilities not repugnant to the laws and constitution of Michigan."[23] The administrative subcommittee accepted William Landman's proposal that the city commission also have the authority to choose the city manager. With those decisions made, it remained for the charter commission to reconcile the respective roles of these two key executive positions, mayor and manager, within the new city charter.

The Preamble

The preamble was the first part of the new charter to be completed, and even though the particulars of the proposed city charter had yet to be fleshed out, its purpose shone through clearly in the preamble. Voicing an array of high-minded administrative ideals, this prefatory statement declared, "We the people of Grand Rapids in order to perfect a municipal government" dedicated to "economic and efficient administration" and the "security of persons and property," to "encourage municipal cooperation among the cities of the state," and to "preserve…the privilege of local self-government do ordain and establish this charter."[24]

The language was as firmly rooted in the city's immediate past as any abstract notions of perfect municipal government. The sentiments expressed in the preamble made good sense in light of events dating from the strikebound summer of 1911. In the wake of the West Side riot at the Widdicomb factory, the issue of security of persons and property had made regular appearances in the furniture trade journals, the mayoral campaigns, and the literature of the Good Government League.

The image of a city exposed to "anarchists" and unruly foreign elements – as well as the dramatic showing by a Socialist mayoral candidate – preyed on the minds of industrialists and bankers, just as Ellis's appointment of striking workers as special policemen continued to rankle representatives of the city's propertied interests. When an editorial in the *Herald* voiced a demand for law and order above all else, manufacturers applauded the paper for the only time during the entire strike; indeed it was the only time that the manufacturers praised any of the city's newspapers during that tension-filled year.[25]

Although there had been complaints and calls for investigation of Ellis's decision to move city funds from one department to another during the 1913-14 recession, for the most part there were few complaints about the fiscal administration of the city. Tax revenues were steady, bond issues were conservatively limited to sewers and school improvements, and Moody's continued to rate the city as AAA.[26] There were no scandals of misplaced funds, overpriced purchases, or shoddy construction such as the disgraceful water scandal of 1901. Rather, the statement contained in the preamble was a coded way of decrying aldermanic politics. It was not that the city was run poorly from the perspective of outsiders such as the investors represented by Moody's manual. Instead, the issue of security for persons and property echoed the manufacturers' lingering concerns over the attacks on their factories, their strike-breakers, and their persons during the 1911 strike.

Finally, the preamble's call for cooperation among cities was a response to emerging Progressive strategies for the purchase of materials and bidding for government contracts. A municipal league could buy in volume and help regulate the cost of government.[27] Interest in inter-municipal cooperation also reflected the experience of the Grand Rapids Good Government League, which had joined its efforts with the Detroit chapter and merged in the publication of a single newspaper by 1906, and sought to secure a consensus for dealing with moral issues and immoral politicians.[28]

The preamble to the proposed charter served an important purpose: It advertised the concerns animating the reformers and stood in contrast to the realities of current city government. The preamble also set forth the principles guiding the charter commissioners' efforts and allowed them to move along to the next phase of work – constructing a new government that would more completely embody those concerns of political power and principle.

The Power of Patronage

As they proceeded in their deliberations, the charter commission members attacked the practice of patronage that in its most significant form had helped Ellis and other political bosses hold power, and attempted to replace it with a competitive civil service system.[29] Under the new system, they proposed that temporary jobs on the city payroll – that mainstay of ward heelers – would no longer be handed out as political favors to out-of-work constituents as had been the case in 1914. Instead, the charter commission declared, "By a system of registration and otherwise, the Commissioners shall make rules and regulations concerning the employment of common laborers which shall require…such employment to originate on merit and to continue during good behavior."

This mandate to employ meritorious, well-behaved workers further diminished the mayor's and aldermen's political base by giving "preference to residents of the city who are citizens of the United States." The majority of non-naturalized immigrants, most of them Polish, would be cut off at once – and for some time following – from the kind of city-based patronage jobs, such as paving streets, cleaning up parks, and digging sewer lines, that had supported the West Side in times of crisis, or even during periods of normal growth. This new approach would break the cycle that had permitted Ellis and others to build successful coalitions based on working-class needs.

Although they had attacked Ellis's use of patronage in support of unskilled and non-naturalized residents, the reformers essentially replaced one pool of favored recipients with another by creating unclassified and classified categories of jobs.[30] The unclassified posts included all elected officials, the city manager, heads of departments, appointed boards, and the city manager's staff. In these cases, professional competence presumably preceded appointment. The classified service referred to "all positions not specifically included...in the unclassified service." These posts fell into competitive, noncompetitive, and labor categories. The competitive class covered all positions where "it is practicable to determine the merit and fitness of applicants by competitive examination." The pool for this job-seeking group would naturally favor applicants with skills in mathematics and familiarity with English. The children of immigrants might aspire to these posts, but only the educated would be able to compete, and they would face stiff competition.[31]

The appearance of fairness created by the large pool of competitive civil service jobs was belied by the noncompetitive class, which actually enlarged the number of positions available for the commissioners to fill. Reserved for the commissioners to dispense at their discretion were all positions "requiring peculiar and exceptional qualifications of a scientific, managerial, professional or educational character as may be determined by the rules of the Board." In effect, the well-educated sons of industrialists, bankers, and lawyers, rather than factory workers, now had some chance of employment in city service. Service board members were also to be appointed by the commissioners and automatically exempt from any sort of competitive exams. Further, the charter was silent on the staffing of key service boards and left to others the task of deciding which posts within each department would be competitive or noncompetitive.

Labor was the final group in the unclassified category. Here, too, the new rules requiring laborers working for the city to be born or naturalized citizens militated against the West Side immigrant community. According to the federal census of 1910, the highest rate of non-naturalization occurred among the Poles, who were also most likely to live on the West Side and hold down unskilled jobs.

Civil service reform as laid out in the proposed charter did not put an end to political patronage; it merely changed the pool of acceptable patronage recipients and eliminated brokering between the mayor and the aldermen over appointments to city hall. By giving the city commission power over the direct appointment or removal of municipal officials, the charter made the commissioners alone the ultimate dispensers of patronage.

The charter commission's attempt to create a civil service system came at the same time that commission members adopted a proposal to reduce the number of wards from twelve to three.[32] By so doing, they not only divided the city into three numerically equal camps, but also effectively diluted the strength of Dutch and Polish immigrant voters. The entire West Side was melded into a single ward – the First Ward – while the east side of the river was divided into two wards; the Second Ward reached from Wealthy Street northward and the Third Ward extended from Wealthy Street south.

The consolidation of the wards was a major step toward the concentration of power in the hands of a proposed new seven-member city commission dominated by the East Side's Second and Third wards, where business and industry leaders exercised greater control. With two members elected from each ward and a seventh at-large commissioner (the mayor), the East Side was all but guaranteed possession of a working majority in every debatable issue. Leaders of the Third Ward's hilltop community would be in a position to exercise greater political power over the stubborn Netherlanders on Grandville Avenue and, simultaneously, look after the affairs of what had previously been the Eleventh Ward to the city's southeast. The Second Ward would combine the blue-collar residents in the city's north end with a portion of the hilltop and middle-class families along the city's eastern edge, diluting the impact of the area that had been the stronghold of the Socialist vote in the 1912 mayoral campaign.

With the commission structure, ward plan, and civil service system outlined in detail, the charter commission turned its attention to the executive office, seeking to place more authority in the hands of a city manager at the expense of the mayor. By summer's end a majority of the commissioners had agreed to do away with the mayor as anything more than a figurehead. Complying with Michigan law, the proposed new charter stated that "insofar as required by law, and for all ceremonial purposes, the mayor shall be recognized as the executive head of the city. He shall exercise only such powers as the state laws, this Charter, or the City Commission specifically confer upon him." As first among equals among his fellow commissioners, the mayor was granted the privilege of voting in city commission meetings, but not accorded the traditional power of executive veto. The city manager would now be responsible for executing the policies and directives of the city commission.

Next, the charter commission board turned to other political offices, such as the police and fire commissioners, that had previously acted independently of commission approval. If the voters endorsed the charter revision, these offices would come under direct city commission supervision, effectively ending all remnants of political patronage. Debate would later erupt over whether the commission could assume both legislative and executive functions at the expense of the mayor, but for the moment traditional mayoral leadership was doomed.

Further evidence that memories of the 1911 strike lay at the heart of many of the reforms appeared in a proposal to create a Department of Public Safety. Before it was removed from the working draft of the charter, the proposed department would have placed in the hands of the city commissioners the ultimate authority to use force against threatened disruption. "In the event that any city commissioner shall determine that riot, public danger or emergency is imminent or exists," the proposal read, "he shall himself or through the City Clerk issue a call for the assembling of the City Commission within six hours of issuing the call." The commission would then determine what measures to take, and "any member or members of the City Commission who meet in response to such a call shall constitute a quorum." These individuals alone would decide what "constitutes a riot, public danger or emergency." In short, the reformers were trying to make sure there would be no repetition of Ellis's dawdling over the violence on the West Side, no chance for strikers to intimidate strikebreakers at the railroad depot or chase them home through the streets. Scenes of the late summer of 1911 would not be repeated. Nor would organized labor's "special interests" jeopardize the welfare of "the people."

Composing the Commission

As the summer of 1915 drew to a close, only one unfinished point remained before the proposed charter could be presented to the voters of Grand Rapids. Given the central importance of the newly defined city commissioners and their possession of both legislative and administrative power, it remained to be determined how these commissioners were to be nominated and elected. As the subcommittee's initial proposal stood, commissioners would be nominated at large, but could be voted for only by the ward they sought to represent.

Two members of the four-man charter commission judiciary subcommittee, Stanley Jackowski, who had been Mayor Ellis's personal secretary, and Daniel Kelley, a printer working for the *Evening Press,* contended that the election and nomination of commissioners must be all one thing or all the other, entirely ward-based or completely at large. Jackowski and Kelley had opposed reducing the mayor to a figurehead and enhancing the post of city manager, and now they saw at-large election as a move to disconnect commissioners from the wards they served. The other members of the subcommittee, and members of the charter commission generally, complained that the proposed selection procedure of at-large nominations combined with ward-only elections limited the electors' choices and was therefore unconstitutional. "These charter provisions," the proposal's critics maintained, "abridge the right of the elective franchise in that they restrict the voters of the city at large in their choice of their representatives.... The elector may think that four or five candidates who live in one ward would be the most desirable officials and yet he is restricted to his voting to two because not more than two can be elected from any one ward."

Although they sought to limit the centralization of power and enhance what was left of representative government, Jackowski and Kelley undermined their own position and inadvertently helped advocates of at-large nomination and election get a hearing. Ultimately, the issue came down to a direct vote that split the charter commission down the middle, and the completely at-large interpretation carried by a single vote.

The battle to circumscribe the centralized government did not end there, however, as the judiciary subcommittee once again raised a legal argument about the combination of both legislative and administrative functions in the city commission. Fred Geib, Stanley Jackowski, and Daniel Kelley all complained that making the city manager a chief executive appointed by the commissioners and subject to removal by them violated the separation of powers. They contended, the mayor, elected by all the people, should be the chief executive, and the commission should act only in a legislative capacity.

However, a minority report of the judiciary subcommittee filed by Henry Jewell argued that the system did not pose any conflict with the state constitution, the Home Rule Act, or the principle of separation of powers. "The proposed charter provides for a system of city government," he wrote, "similar to the system of management of well organized business corporations." Cigar manufacturer William Hensler concurred, stating "There is nothing incongruous or conflicting in the provisions made for in this system...."[33] The city commission would merely act as a board of directors, creating policy, guiding growth, and managing resources. Like Jewell and Hensler, most of the charter commissioners envisioned an orderly new government patterned after a corporation rather than a messy reflection of the ups and downs of representative democracy.

Mayoral Politics

The proposed charter was not presented for public approval until the summer of 1916. Meanwhile, a springtime election brought mayoral politics back to the fore. Incumbent George Ellis, running for an unprecedented sixth consecutive term, lost after the closest contest in the city's history. The morning after the polls closed, Ellis trailed by fewer than 200 votes out of more than 19,000 cast. His opponent, Democrat George P. Tilma, the former city treasurer who had confronted Ellis in 1914 over inter-fund borrowing, managed to cut into Ellis's usually strong support from West Side constituents and emerged victorious. Critical votes came from the expanding Eleventh Ward on the city's Southeast Side, dominated by second-generation Dutch and middle-class wage earners.

Ellis's popularity had been slipping ever since the decisive Democratic inroads in the hotly contested election of 1912. Two years later, what should have been an easy win for him proved to be a race to the wire against Malcolm Sinclair, a nonpartisan candidate sponsored by the Morals Efficiency Commission, who had edged out George Perry in the Democratic primary. Sinclair favored prohibition, reduced taxes, and an end to Ellis's "arraying of class against class" to stay in power. Foreshadowing reform trends that would emerge on the 1915 charter commission, he asserted that "municipal government is a business, not politics," implying that disruption in society was as costly as conflict in the workplace.[34] Sinclair shared the businessman's view that government should be run as an efficient, top-down corporation, not through the contentious give and take of democracy.

Ellis countered Sinclair's conservative stance by declaring his "progressive" concern for the average workingman. Although he maintained his moderate stand on saloon licensing, Ellis was more than willing to buy a round for the house when he visited West Side saloons. Further, he advocated housing codes to improve worker housing and an eight-hour workday for city employees. While Sinclair attacked him for diverting city funds into parks and other public works jobs during the 1913-14 economic downturn, Ellis reminded voters of the jobs he had created, bringing many voters back to the fold. To draw middle-class supporters, he continued a long-standing campaign to maintain municipal financial responsibility by subjecting private utilities to municipal regulation.[35]

But his past efforts were not enough to earn George Ellis reelection in 1916. This time, his opponent was too effective and the issues too volatile. Tilma denied charges that he would impose Sunday blue laws keeping the theaters dark or that he would push through prohibition ordinances forever closing the saloons. Rather, he aimed "to tear down class prejudices built up to further [the] political aspirations" of George Ellis. "We have had too much of this arraying labor against capital," said Tilma, sounding a familiar note. The Democratic candidate went on to plead for a united Grand Rapids under a sound "business administration, guided by nonpartisan principles."[36] In the end Tilma's Dutch ancestry gave him the edge in a city whose Dutch immigrant population had continued to increase faster than any other group.[37]

When the votes had been counted and Tilma's razor-thin election confirmed, even the *Evening Press,* usually a strong Ellis advocate, chided the former mayor for his many "stupid acts" while in office. "The harm he has caused has been due to the fact that he has never scrupled to array citizen against citizen, faction against faction, and class against class whenever it suited his personal ambition," thundered an editorial. "The bitterness and dissension he engendered has more than balanced his public service as an administrator." Here was another, less favorable, recognition of the shifting coalitions that Ellis had put together on an election-by-election, issue-by-issue basis. Instead of seeing Ellis as a leader responsive to the changing needs of the city's various, competing groups, or as a skilled middleman working to reduce conflict, the *Evening Press* assailed him as someone who created and exploited differences. Ellis had gone from facilitator to agitator.

With the city's major papers turned against him, Ellis desperately sought an explanation for his loss. He felt sure that the defeat had come at the price of fair play, and he urged repeal of a provision of the current charter that prevented a lame-duck council from either conducting a recount or invalidating the election. Ellis eventually charged the administration of Calvin College with registering its students to vote, a rather unlikely possibility since the school was the seat of the highly scrupulous and conspicuously ineffective Dutch political society, *Fas et Jus.* For nearly two months after the election, Ellis fought with the council, the city clerk, and the newspapers over the issue of recount and voter invalidation. Finally, at the end of May, Ellis withdrew his appeals from state courts and conceded defeat to George P. Tilma.[38]

The storm of mayoral politics had barely spent its force when city treasurer James Hawkins emerged as the principal suspect in an abuse-of-office scandal.

Charges ranged from embezzlement to the illegal sale of tax-distressed properties. The newly elected council authorized the city attorney to proceed with impeachment proceedings, and for the rest of the summer the Hawkins investigation was fodder for the daily papers. Legal ground blurred when it became uncertain whether the council members or a grand jury should swear out a charge of impeachment. The affair ended in September when Hawkins became ill and the council let him retire gracefully from the scene.[39] The timing of the scandal helped feed the push for charter eform.

Just as the Hawkins affair faded, another crisis arose. Throughout the summer of 1916, an "arson trust" menaced a variety of public and private property in the city. By the beginning of August, twenty fires of suspicious origin had caused damages exceeding $300,000, a sum equal to approximately $5.5 million today. The Imperial Furniture Company sustained damage to its warehouse and dry lumber sheds on three separate occasions. The Valley City Chair Company's main plant was set ablaze at an estimated loss of $125,000, and the downtown Ashton Building, an office complex, suffered damages exceeding $75,000.[40] While not as disruptive to the community as the furniture workers strike five years earlier, the combination of arson and corruption created an environment that put voters in the mood for reform.

The New Charter Election

The campaign for the new charter began in early August. While all the newspapers endorsed the plans for a new city government, the *Herald* went the furthest, running a series of articles exploring the proposed changes section by section and explaining the virtues of centralized government. Frank M. Sparks, the paper's political correspondent, argued in his first installment that the narrow defeat of the 1912 charter proposal proved there was a desire for change, and that the charter now under consideration would provide it.

Sparks emphasized in his articles those parts of the charter that dealt with taxation, public and special improvements, municipal franchises to utilities, and the sinking fund. These areas of rather technical and somewhat obtuse language beyond the average reader, he explained, offered "distinct and radical departures...from our present Charter." Avoiding the broader issues of political control and the near absolute authority given to the commission members, Sparks emphasized the same pouints concerning governmental efficiency referred to in endorsements by the Association of Commerce and the Good Government League.

To those voters whose concerns centered on moral rather than fiscal questions, Sparks intimated that the new charter would protect existing saloon owners while likely curbing future growth. "Under the proposed new charter, the city will still continue to be conservative in the number of licenses to be granted," he assured readers. But while today "we are conservative by action of the council only," the new charter would see that "conservatism is made mandatory" and not subject to the partisan politics that had been so divisive in the city's past. In other words, objective principles would guide the issuance of saloon licenses in Grand Rapids. The new charter would keep the ratio of saloons to residents at 1:700, slightly fewer than the 1:500 prescribed by state law. In reality, as the city's population grew, the ratio diminished to 1:800 by 1920.

The only consistent opposition to the new charter came from Fred Geib, a member of the judiciary subcommittee. During the committee's deliberations, he had argued against the at-large election of commissioners. He saw the proposed government as one of enhanced privilege centered into fewer hands and subject to fewer checks and balances than the older mayoral system. In a lengthy statement made at the time the commission adopted the proposed charter, he maintained that the intense concentration of power provided by the charter opened the door to easy abuse of public services such as gas, water, and rail. The new charter did not "protect the people against a corrupted city commission and a misled electorate with reference to the enormous values in the streets of the city, which I claim inherently belong to the community," argued Geib. The "people who create the values" of these public properties would be easily exploited by "special interests" without any safeguard to stop the abuse. But Geib's arguments never appeared at length outside the charter commission and showed up only once in the *Herald.*

On August 29, 1916, voters went to the polls knowing little about the nature of the proposed charter. Arguments favoring ratification had appeared daily in all the papers, but they were confined to promises of efficient government and detailed discussions of bonding procedures. Only those few voters who had actually read the charter understood the immense power it concentrated in the commission's hands and the latitude given for its use. Despite the lack of an effective opposition campaign, the final vote was close, with the charter winning acceptance by 7,693 to 6,021, a margin of slightly more than five percent of the total votes cast.[41]

The business community wasted no time boasting of its role in securing the winning margin. Claiming credit for its participation in the reform movement from the very beginning, the Association of Commerce also noted that, as a rule, it never got involved in politics. In this case, its leaders argued, the association merely helped to assure a "charter commission [was] authorized" by the voters and then continued its work through the explicitly political Good Government League. It was the league's activities, "largely financed by the members of the Association of Commerce," that ultimately secured adoption of the new charter. Trying to avoid the label of "special interest," the association argued that it was "merely a group of citizens" involved in the city's welfare, helping to promote the change. "Securing a new charter for the city was a matter of business and not politics."[42]

The association's denial was unconvincing. From the outset, businessmen had been determined to extend their control over the city, and after earlier false starts, this time they engaged in politics with a skill that matched their organizational abilities in the marketplace. Although they maintained that "business" was devoid of any interest except the maximization of profit for the objectively run corporation, the reformers' motives were political from the outset, and no amount of denial could change that reality. In the name of efficiency, the new charter replaced the democratic inefficiencies of compromise and brokered deals with a newer, centralized, corporate-like administration.

A close look at the ward and precinct voting patterns tells the story of how the new charter vote passed. The Second, Third, and Tenth wards provided enthusiastic support for the proposed changes. Here lived the industrialists, lawyers, and bankers who formed the leadership of the Furniture Manufacturers Association, the Employers Association, and the Association of Commerce. These men shared social and business connections through Kent Country Club and the Peninsular Club, and many were members of Fountain Street Baptist Church where Reverend Wishart lectured on the wisdom of industrial leadership in politics. These solid citizens were the driving force behind the new charter effort.

The Fourth, Fifth, and Eleventh wards along the East Side filled out the ranks of pro-charter support. Families that had come to the area from New England, New York, and Canada, together with second-generation Dutch, lived in this part of the city. Some worked for the furniture factories, and their peers had jobs in other industries around town. Many in the southeastern Eleventh Ward were clerks, salesmen, or small businessmen. While these voters did not display the enthusiasm for the charter held by their neighbors in the hilltop precincts and turned out in proportionately fewer numbers, they did endorse the charter.

Pointing to ethnic and class divisions in the charter vote, the immigrant and working-class West Side, joined by the Twelfth Ward on the Southwest Side, voted almost to a precinct against the sweeping charter changes. The West Side ethnic and class pattern appeared again along the city's eastern edge where Poles from the brickyard neighborhood and immigrant Dutch in the Second Ward registered their dissent at the ballot boxes. The most intense repudiation of the proposed charter came from the Sixth and Seventh wards in the northwestern corner of Grand Rapids, which held the largest concentration of Poles and Lithuanians in the city and the second largest group of immigrant Dutch. Residents here were wage earners in the furniture factories and had been the backbone of the strike in 1911. They had determined that the new charter was not in their best interests, but their vote was not enough to overcome the support the charter received throughout most of the East Side.

After a decade of struggle, the furniture manufacturers and other economic leaders of the new industrial city finally controlled the government. They owed at least a portion of their victory to issues of ethnicity, class, and religious fragmentation that worked to splinter wage earners' cohesion. The number and diversity of immigrants to the industrial city was at its height in the years after 1900, and efforts at municipal reform came at a time when this diversity was most pronounced.[43] At times, workers literally did not speak the same language. The Dutch Calvinists' experience suggested that even in neighborhoods where immigrants shared a common language, other issues such as provincial rivalries and theological disputes could tear apart an ethnic community. In this regard, they were similar to groups voting on municipal reform in other American cities. Diverse religious loyalties tore at the Germans of Pittsburgh, and provincial differences divided Italian immigrants in Cleveland.[44]

Fragmentation along ethnic and religious lines cannot entirely explain the success of charter reform in Grand Rapids. Manufacturers had to convince voters that reform was in their interest and find enough support from working-class neighborhoods to forge a majority. One major factor contributing to the endorsement of reform by wage earners was the high degree of home owner-ship in Grand Rapids. The commitment to home ownership and the family life it represented created a fear of disruption. The 1916 charter stressed a promise of stability through efficient, businesslike administration. By accepting this em-phasis on the security of property, homeowners across the city found common cause with the industrialists.[45]

This commitment to private property, combined with religious and ethnic fragmentation, divided workers in Grand Rapids. The unrelieved disruption in the years after 1910 only exacerbated these divisions. Given the context of local politics, the manufacturers' program of reform presented voters with an alter-nate strategy for preserving their material gains while participating in the political process. The irony was that workers contributed to their own political exclusion by voting for the new commission-manager government.

Endnotes

1. *Furniture Manufacturer and Artisan,* vol. 63 (August, 19, 1911), p. 424.
2. *Michigan Tradesman,* vol. 50 (April 26, 1933), p. 24; *Furniture Manufacturer and Artisan,* op. cit., p. 426.
3. Martin J. Schiesl, *The Politics of Efficiency: Municipal Administration and Reform in America 1880-1920* (Berkeley, 1972), pp. 46-67.
4. *Grand Rapids Evening Press,* February 21, 1912, p. 6; *Grand Rapids Herald,* February 20, 1912, p. 4.
5. *Herald,* February 20, 1912, p. 6; February 22, 1912, p. 3.
6. Anthony Travis, "Mayor George Ellis: Grand Rapids' Political Boss and Progressive Reformer," *Michigan History* 58 (Spring, 1974), pp. 101-30; Good Government League, "Sidelights on George Ellis," "George Ellis as Juggler," "Repudiated by Republicans: Ellis Has Never Received the Full Vote of the Party" (Grand Rapids: Good Government League, 1914-1916).
7. *Herald,* March 30, 1912, p. 6.
8. Travis, "Mayor George Ellis," *Michigan History;* election returns in *Herald,* April 2, 1912, p. 6.
9. *Herald,* April 2, 1912, p. 6; February 12, 1912, p. 3.
10. See Chapter 2 for a fuller description of the North End neighborhoods.
11. Nationally, members of the Socialist Party were drawn from native-born Americans, a fact mirrored in the 1912 mayoral election. See Gerald Rosenblum, *Immigrant Workers: Their Impact on American Labor Radicalism* (New York: Basic Books, 1973), especially pp. 151-53 in the chapter "The Myth of Immigrant Radicalism." Also useful is Nathan Fine, *Labor and Farmer Parties in the United States* (New York: Rand School of Social Science, 1928), and John S. MacDonald, "Urbanization, Ethnic Groups and Social Segmentation," *Social Research* 29 (Winter, 1962), p. 434.
12. Analysis of citywide data based on tax books, 1909-1912; *Supplement to the 1920 Federal Census.*
13. Ernest M. Fisher and Raymond F. Smith, "Land Subdividing and the Rate of Utilization," *Michigan Business Studies* 4 (1932), pp. 454-532.
14. Frank M. Sparks, *The Business of Government Municipal Reform* (Chicago: n.p., 1916).
15. *Grand Rapids City Charter,* 1916.
16. Travis, "Mayor George Ellis," *Michigan History,* p. 121.
17. Grand Rapids Good Government League, "George Ellis as Juggler," (n.d.); on the debate about accounting procedures, see Schiesl, *op. cit.,* pp. 88-110; Herbert Stein, *The Fiscal Revolution in America* (Chicago: University of Chicago Press, 1969), pp. 6-38; Men like Ellis operated proto-public works programs on the local level, and many working-class constituents knew how it was financed and endorsed it. For a more complete description, see John D. Buenker, *Urban Liberation and Progressive Reform* (New York: Scribner, 1973).
18. Schiesl, op. cit., pp. 88-110.
19. *Grand Rapids Progress,* Vol. 5 (October 1916), p. 16.
20. Minutes of the Board of Directors, Grand Rapids Board of Trade, January 12, 1915, p. 8.
21. *Grand Rapids Progress,* Vol. 4 (January, 1915), p. 14.
22. *City Directory of Grand Rapids,* 1912; residential property taxes in city tax books.
23. Minutes of the Charter Commission, City of Grand Rapids, 1915, bound carbon copy of typescript original in Michigan Room, Grand Rapids Public Library, May 5, 1915, pp. 25-26; May 11, 1915, p. 32; May 25, 1915, p. 48; June 1, 1915, pp. 57-58
24. Grand Rapids City Charter of 1916.
25. *Herald,* May 16, 1911, p. 4.
26. Moody's Manual of Municipal Bonds, 1922.
27. Schiesl, op. cit.; Rice, op. cit.
28. Raymond Fragnoli, "Progressive Coalitions and Municipal Reform: Charter Revision in Detroit 1912-1918," *Detroit in Perspective* 4 (Spring, 1980), pp. 119-42.
29. Schiesl, op. cit.; Rice, op. cit.; Minutes, June 2, 1915, p. 63.
30. Minutes of the Charter Commission, August 31, 1915, p. 105, 109; September 7, 1915, pp. 115-22; Schiesl, *op. cit.*

31. From 1916-1934, city commissioners also served as examining members of the Civil Service Board, Frank J. Schulte, "Municipal Personnel Administration: City of Grand Rapids," 1970. The few competitive exams given in the years 1916-1934 were the Army Alpha Tests that discriminated against immigrants and others who had not been educated in the Anglo-American tradition. For a popular history of the intelligence tests of the Progressive Era see Stephen Jay Gould, *The Mismeasure of Man* (New York: W. W. Norton & Company, 1982).

32. Minutes of the Charter Commission, June 2, 1915, p. 63; June 15, 1915, pp. 73-74.

33. Ibid. September 7, 1915, p. 122; January 12, 1916, pp. 388-89; January 19, 1916, p. 392; January 25, 1916, p. 398.

34. *Herald*, April 4, 1916, pp. 1-2; 6; Travis, op. cit., pp. 120-23.

35. Travis, op. cit., p. 123.

36. *Herald,* April 4, 1916, p. 2.

37. Travis, op. cit., p. 129.

38. *Grand Rapids Evening Press,* April 4, 1916, p. 6; April 8, 1916, p. 1; May 30, 1916, p. 14.

39. Z.Z. Lydens, *The Story of Grand Rapids,* 1966, p. 68.

40. *Herald,* August 6, 1916, p. 1.

41. Ibid. August 19, 1916, p. 5; August 20, 1916. p. 1, 4; August 27, 1916, p. 4; *Press,* August 30, 1916, p. 1.

42. *Grand Rapids Progress,* vol. 5 (October, 1916), p. 16; vol. 6 (May, 1917), p. 15.

43. David Ward, *Cities and Immigrants: A Geography of Change in Nineteenth Century* (New York: Oxford University Press, 1971).

44. Josef Bartow, *Peasants and Strangers: Italians, Rumanians and Slovaks in an American City* (Cambridge: Harvard University Press, 1975); Nora Faires, "Ethnicity in Evolution: The German Community in Pittsburgh and Allegheny City, Pennsylvania 1845-1885" (Ph. D. dissertation, University of Pittsburgh, 1981).

45. Richard Sennett, *Families Against the City: Middle-Class Homes of Industrial Chicago: 1872-1890* (Cambridge: Harvard University Press, 1970).

Chapter 7

A League of Their Own:
Businessmen, Bankers, and the Limits of Control

With the successful charter election in the spring of 1916, the businessmen and bankers of Grand Rapids transformed municipal government into a vehicle subject to their influence. Now, needing a way to protect their charter victory and promote their political agenda, they established the Grand Rapids Citizens League. The newly organized league, having many of the same members and leaders as the earlier Citizens Alliance, operated over the next seven years as a powerful advocate for the city's business and financial interests. Its founders never regarded direct democracy a useful model for their organization. In the new scheme of things, the voters were no longer considered shareholders to whom the government was accountable, but bystanders removed from the governing process. The city would be a closed corporation and the league would serve as its guardian.

A Closed Corporation

Well funded and well organized, the Grand Rapids Citizens League was created in the winter of 1916-17 to ensure the "election of qualified officials" to the city commission.[1] Among its earliest tasks was to defend against legal challenges to the charter that had begun immediately after the election and to provide enough manpower to review petitions from voters demanding a re-examination of the new city government. Established to protect the city's "modern, businesslike" government, the league resembled nothing so much as a business itself, with a centralized decision-making board, a principal secretary to coordinate and execute the board's policy decisions, and a staff of workers to assist the secretary.

In the winter of 1916, as the business community looked ahead to its first test of strength under the new charter – the election of the seven-member city commission – former mayor Carroll F. Sweet wrote to the newly formed league's leaders from his offices in the Old National Bank building, the same location as the league's offices. "The object to be obtained is the election of seven commissioners whom any man would feel proud to have act as a board of directors for his own business." Reflecting the opinion of many businessmen, Sweet went on to assert that because "the city is the largest corporation in this community and that its business is the most important," its board of directors, the city commission, should be made up of "the most able business brains in this community."[2]

Sweet argued that securing such a slate of seven able men would not be easy because too many unqualified men would seek office just for the money. It was "unfortunate" that the offices under city government actually paid wages because "this alone invites competition...which would otherwise be inconsiderable." A strong organization was essential to fend off the swarm of unqualified and undesirable office seekers and promote those with the right stuff.

Viewing participatory politics as a waste of time, Sweet advocated that the league dispense with any pretense of shared governance by structuring itself along the lines of a closed corporation. For men of his generation, a closed corporation signified a business without public stockholders and answerable only to its directors. Sweet wrote that the "democratic type" of political organization invited disasters, while the closed corporation "will know at its inception that it must pay for what it gets; that it is answerable to no one except itself; that it is not depending for support upon any subsidiary organization...and that it has to deal with no one within its own organization who has personal axes to grind."

Sweet maintained that the league should function under the guidance of an executive committee comprised of such business notables as Clay Hollister, chairman of the board of the Grand Rapids Savings Bank, and Charles W. Garfield, vice president of the Old National Bank and a member of the Grand Rapids Clearing House. Committee members such as these could "get together possibly at a luncheon meeting fifty or one hundred men who would put up a hundred or fifty dollars apiece; who would...nominate a number of men, any seven of whom would be agreeable to them as commissioners, or would create a small executive committee...to select a slate and carry on the business of the organization."[3] In other words, a small, elite leadership should run the league, which would, in turn, direct the work of the seven-member city commission.

Nor should the league's behind-the-scene activities ever be revealed to the general public, declared Sweet. League campaign materials should never be signed, executive committee membership should never be listed, and the public should never learn who paid for the materials. All "such publicity as would be advantageous would be the impersonal, educative type, preferably without source, because [it would] then not [be] subject to the criticisms of personal antagonists to the source itself." Hiding behind a mask of anonymous authority, Sweet and fellow league leaders did not open up their organization to a democratic process, hoping instead to obscure the special interests behind it through "impersonal, educative" literature that encouraged citizens to vote while limiting their choices.

Member Recruitment

At the same time that Sweet was calling for a closed-corporation approach to league affairs, the league's managers sought to build a broader constituency among the city's residents. While they depended on financial support from the men Sweet hoped would be the league's deep pockets, league organizers also solicited memberships and cash donations from the general public. Women were high on their list. Although women had not yet won the right to vote in state or national elections, their strength was growing, and if they received the vote, league officials saw them as an untapped source of voter strength, a new constituency to exploit.

Throughout its existence, fund raising was never far from the top of the league's priority list. During its first fund-raising year, 1916-17, the league received contributions from 280 recorded donors; 42 of the givers were the wives and daughters of industrialists — Blodgett, Garfield, Hollister, and Irwin among them — and their gifts were in the $5 and $10 range.[4]

Setting its sights on a more diverse group of women, the league then reached out via mass mailing to the city's schoolteachers, most of whom were women. The solicitation letter praised good government and active citizenship and then asked the teachers to support these worthy goals by sending in donations of one dollar.[5] While the campaign was not a success, bringing in only about $20, the effort demonstrates the tactics of the league's top officials, who understood the need for aggressively recruiting targeted audiences and using the then-innovative technique of direct-mail solicitation.

The emphasis on courting women became an even more important strategy in the league's campaign efforts after 1918 when women gained the right to vote in Michigan state elections. As league secretary C. Roy Hatten noted later on in a letter to the National Municipal League, "The fact that we had a thorough organization among the new women voters, having obtained several thousand members, coupled with considerable publicity…contributed to the result" of winning commission seats.[6]

The league also took the opportunity during its first year to carpet the city with 5,000 copies of its newspaper, the *Sentinel,* distributed by volunteers. In a time of national crisis, with the United States pledged to enter the war in Europe, the league's call for citizenship and civic duty prompted nearly 1,400 residents to send in donations and sign up for membership. But when peace descended in the fall of 1918, interest declined and more than 700 chose not renew their Citizens League memberships.[7]

Still seeking to expand its membership base, the league turned in February 1919 to two paid recruiters, offering a salary of $30 per week plus 5 percent of the gross receipts, an income on a par with that of a well-paid factory worker.

Once recently returned army officer Lt. Russell Griffen and his partner, L. H. Spade, were on board, they began mapping out an intensive campaign, to begin in March 1919. Their strategy was to divide the city into districts of roughly equal population and then set out, district by district, to sign up league members.[8] Supplementing their footwork were direct mailings, newspaper distribution, and teenage volunteers. In a complimentary letter shortly thereafter, Joel Barlow, president of the Barlow Blank Book Company, noted how willingly he parted with a dollar when confronted with a clean-cut lad whose forceful manner made a convincing case for supporting the league. "I don't know the boy at all," wrote Barlow, "but he makes a clean impression."[9]

A "Reasonable Touch"

For the seven years that it lasted, the Grand Rapids Citizens League claimed a base of economic and political support from "wise voters" who volunteered their time and money to promote good government. In fact, the league was the creature of the city's biggest businesses, and of the businessmen who contributed most of the money that fueled its $12,000 annual operating budget. These contributions bankrolled a full- and part-time crew of workers who staffed a telephone bank, sent out targeted mass mailings, and even watched the polling places during elections to make sure that only "qualified" voters cast their ballots. Regular advertisements in the city's daily papers complemented the Citizens League's weekly news report.

In the continuing quest for support, league leaders asked prominent businessmen to circulate lists of "persons whom you believe would be susceptible to a reasonable touch."[10] Officers of the Wolverine Brass Works submitted a list of potential contributors guaranteed to "bring in close to $20,000," plus a sublist of "$100 men."[11] The league's substantial war chest for 1917 came from a broadly based group of businessmen, of whom 12 of 123 potential donors gave between $500 and $1,000 apiece.[12] While the furniture industry accounted for a significant share of the working capital, the donors' names revealed a wide range of interests, including law, banking, and wholesale and retail trade. According to league records, the first fiscal year produced receipts exceeding $32,000, half of which was spent on daily operations.

It became an article of financial faith that raising as much as $5,000 would "not be difficult, providing the cooperation of a dozen men and women can be secured." The citizenship pitch went out wherever businessmen gathered, including weekly Rotary meetings and the annual Grand Rapids wholesalers banquet. But over time, these approaches yielded diminishing results, and the furniture manufacturers came to play a disproportionate role in sustaining the league. List after list of contributors giving amounts of $100 or more contained the names of such furniture men as Gay, Tietsort, Hompe, Irwin, Wilmarth, Foote, and Sligh, who identified their contributions as coming from their companies rather than themselves.[13]

The business establishment, led by the furniture industry, sustained the league and kept it solvent. Eventually a cadre of thirty men, who could cover "more than half the needed amount" to conduct league activities, ended up providing the money to keep the wheels rolling.[14] One of the core group, John W. Blodgett, tried to ease his self-imposed burden by claiming his contributions were tax deductible. The newly created Internal Revenue Service listened to Blodgett but denied his request. Although the league's efforts were praiseworthy, and the league itself was tax-exempt, the IRS wrote, the organization did not exist "exclusively for religious, charitable, scientific or educational purposes"; nor did it work to prevent "cruelty to animals or children."[15] Controlling the local political scene did not fall under the heading of tax-deductible activities.

Given the lack of widespread economic support among city residents, league officials mulled over the possibility of turning for donations to the various religious groups in town. Almost as an afterthought, league leadership offered the opinion that they should seek "better cooperation from the churches of Grand Rapids" and establish a civic committee in each church's social structure.

In 1923, the league's final year of existence, the finance committee considered hiring a professional fund raiser to secure $30,000 over a five-week drive at a cost of $3,000. After due consideration, the executive board said no.[16]

Reformers vs. Amenders

Despite its initial financial success, the need for continued fund raising dogged the league during its later existence, with most of the money in its coffers going to fight the repeated efforts by various groups to amend the 1916 charter. A lively contest unfolded at the polls nearly every April as Citizens League advocates and supporters and a variety of individuals and groups from around the city argued their respective points of view.

No sooner had the new charter been adopted than opponents attacked the provision that had rendered the mayor a ceremonial figurehead appointed by the city commissioners. These "amenders," never formally organized and drawn together only by their opposition to the charter, wanted the mayor restored to an at-large position, directly elected by the voters and capable of exercising some executive powers. Advocates for initiatives to amend the charter, including former mayor Ellis, union officials, former aldermen, and immigrant leaders, argued that while centralized control and a streamlined city commission might be acceptable, giving the commissioners unlimited executive and legislative authority was too much of a good thing. In the years before 1916, the mayor had acted as a broker for various local interests and served as a check on the city council's power. Even if the council voted to take a particular action, the mayor's job was to enforce, delay, interpret, or temper the council's decisions as he saw fit. And if he did not do a good job, then the mayor was accountable to the entire city electorate, not merely the council.

The loose-knit group that sought to amend the charter also contended the city clerk and the city attorney should not be appointed by the commissioners, but, like the mayor, should be elected at large as a counterbalance to the power exercised by the commissioners. The city clerk dealt with elections, voting regulations, and petitions to the city government, among other things, and could affect the city's political climate by the degree of cooperation shown to ordinary residents seeking advice and assistance. The same could be said for the city attorney, whose principal role was to assure that municipal ordinances did not conflict with state statutes, but who might be willing to do the bidding of the commissioners. As in the call for a directly elected mayor, the key issue here was the accountability of public servants to the broader constituency of the electorate.

Finally, the "amenders" wanted the commissioners to live in and be elected by the wards they represented. Satisfied that fewer representatives might be better, or at least no worse, than the older twelve-ward system, they nevertheless entertained serious doubts that someone who claimed to represent a ward could do so without actually living there. The reformers, on the other hand, had pushed hard for the new at-large system, creating a city commission that would act on behalf of the entire city while hilltop residents dominated its ranks. With time, money, and organization rarely matched by the opponents, the business elite now possessed a distinct advantage in political control, and they had no intention of giving it up.

Nowhere did this attitude show up more strongly than in the first election campaign for commission seats after the new city charter became law in 1917. Mobilizing quickly and aggressively along a variety of fronts, the Citizens League sent out several thousand pamphlets announcing its existence, invited new members to join at dues of 25 cents apiece, and established 28 branch offices in barbershops and drug stores, which were gathering places for men of all ages. The league-endorsed candidates swept to victory. League secretary Hatten wrote that five of the seven candidates were well thought of by the business community and in high standing with that group; the other two, also endorsed by the league, were "more closely in touch with the common people" and thereby permitted some balance to the representative mix. These two were William Oltman, shoe store owner, and Daniel Kelley, president of the Grand Rapids Trades and Labor Council; both men had served on the original commission that drafted the charter under which they were elected.[17]

As a result of its successful election campaign and sizeable treasury, the league attracted attention in other parts of the state. Members of the Detroit Citizens League wanted to know how the Grand Rapids men had done the job. Secretary Hatten replied that although former mayor Ellis "played all his old tricks and more new ones" in the canvass, the league, relying on an "airtight organization," beat him at his own game.[18] Success involved conducting a neighborhood grass-roots survey to find sympathetic voters and then assuring their timely arrival at the polls. "I made a house-to-house canvass of the City," explained Hatten, "to secure lines on...League votes which were alphabetically indexed and put in the voting place in each precinct."

On election day Hatten secured "two Calvin College boys in each precinct as challengers to check these votes" to assure that those who had promised to vote had actually done so. If the promised voters did not appear by noon, then league precinct watchers compiled lists of the absentees on the basis of street addresses and handed them to "our personal workers" outside the polls with instructions to fetch the errant voters and encourage the exercise of their franchise. "Two or more automobiles in each precinct," Hatten noted, were available to bring the "missing persons" to the voting places.

The system was also used in later elections. At one point, Hatten circulated letters stating the need for "60-70 autos after 1:00 p.m. on election day April 5, 1920." Automobile volunteers were told to "pay particular attention to the women voters, and by TACT and DIPLOMACY try to get them to vote. DON'T SCOLD. Get them to get their men to vote on the way home or after supper."[19]

The league also mobilized naturalized immigrant families by sending speakers to public and parochial elementary and high schools where they exhorted students to check on their parents to be sure that they had voted. Each voter was to be "tagged" at the polls, and students were to collect these tags as evidence of their family's participation. Attempting to motivate the youngsters through peer pressure, the league promised prizes for those schools with the greatest number of tags in proportion to the size of the school's precinct and ward.[20]

The league also tried to manipulate public opinion by leaking information to the noon editions of the local newspapers. Playing on traditional ethnic, religious, and class rivalries, Hatten "threw a scare" into East Side residents by reporting that West Side voting was heavy and East Side voting was light. In fact, that was not the case at all, but by releasing the misleading information, "We routed the sleeping ones out and put votes in the box and won...."

With ample funds at the league's disposal, publicity drove the first campaign. Newspaper advertising, free pamphlets distributed around the city, and "other novel methods" carried the league's message. Lapel buttons sprouted everywhere. "An educational exhibit was opened on the main thoroughfare, exhibiting in detail our city government and the new charter," and "pictures of our candidates were run in the downtown moving picture houses." In the face of the unprecedented media blitz, few voters remained unexposed to the league candidates.[21]

Getting Out the Vote

In the years after 1917, the league needed a steady flow of money and publicity to keep its organizational drive effective and its ability to locate and deliver voters secure. In its ongoing effort to get out the vote, the league installed a bank of ten telephones at which sat ten "girls" who called every number in the phone book. While small and labor intensive by current standards, the operation demonstrated the resourcefulness of the league's leaders in creating and maintaining contacts with potential supporters. Receiving the names of members of clubs and fraternal organizations, including some 2,000 members of various Odd Fellows Lodges in Grand Rapids, was also something "we can certainly use to good advantage," wrote Hatten, "and it will be greatly appreciated."[22]

In another get-out-the-vote tactic, the league urged "large retailers and business houses to allow all voters in their employ to vote before 5:30 when the factories close," presuming the grateful workers would vote the "right way" if they were permitted to go to the polls at midday rather than after work.[23] In April 1921, bothered by the fact that only one-sixth of all registered voters went to the polls for an important primary election, the league's executive committee exhorted members: "You can help overcome this lack of interest in self-government by urging at least ten acquaintances to go to the polls and vote next Monday."[24] Two years later, in an ongoing effort to police the polls and the voters, the league secretary announced with "great pleasure" the "completion of our card index system which includes every registered voter in the city of Grand Rapids." The master file, consisting of 24 trays and 45,000 cards, had been compiled with the help of the city clerk.[25]

On those rare occasions when league candidates won by uncomfortably close margins, blame fell on the failure to turn out the vote — or at least the "right" voters. In 1918, when former mayor George Ellis made something of a comeback and secured the at-large commission seat, Hatten fumed that "we succeeded in getting out [only] two of five of the registered voters…at the polls." But turning out the vote required regular and sizable amounts of money, and it became the conventional wisdom that lack of money spelled failure at the ballot box. Hatten made this point early in the league's history when he wrote to the Detroit Citizens League that, without a budget of $2,200 to influence the nomination of candidates and $5,000 for the actual election, "I am satisfied that we should have been defeated."[26]

Money Talks

Money and organization rested at the heart of the league's activities. Municipal elections were held in the spring, and a cycle of meetings beforehand brought key league committees together on an average of once a week, alternating the formats between working lunches and sitting down at the league offices. Occasionally a "spontaneous" meeting of concerned citizens could be arranged to voice support for the new city charter and the government it created.[27] Each year, the three months before the spring election saw a flurry of meetings, pledge drives, lists of canvassers, and polling-place checkers and challengers, designed to assure victory for league-supported candidates.

None of this came cheap. Disbursements in the municipal elections of 1917 and 1919 included $1,214.66 in standard advertising costs in the daily papers; $353.25 for challengers to verify voter credentials at the polls; and funds to cover the printing and distribution of handbills, only $1.50 of which was spent on printing Polish-language circulars. Other costs included $25 for phone installation at league offices and money for precinct-level canvassers, including $18 each for "2 or more men of Holland descent to make house-to-house canvass in Holland precincts." The league also spent $56.95 for 39 Boy Scouts at 25 cents per hour to blanket the entire city with 17,000 copies of the league's newspaper, the *Sentinel.* The allocation of resources emphasized all but the Polish neighborhoods, focusing instead on those voters perceived as most sympathetic to the businessmen's cause.

In order to reward loyalty and keep reliable help, the league kept a file of all those individuals who would be called upon to serve at each election. Lists of "candidates for service at the election next spring" could run up to three pages long, and opportunities were available to serve as "gate keepers," "inspectors," and "clerks." The city clerk and commissioners appointed these official electoral posts, relying on the league's lists and thereby giving official sanction to its strategy of rewarding "good citizenship."[28]

Most intriguing of all was the fact that the league hired a full time writer to submit letters to the editors of the daily newspapers, salting the mine of public opinion. For two years, the league's hired pen was Charles B. Magennis, a street-wise political operative who had worked for George Ellis and was familiar with all the angles of ward- and precinct-level politics. In the months before an election, Magennis turned out thousands of words in what he called "educational articles" for the league. To insure their continued utility, he suggested that the pieces remain undated and perhaps shortened a bit. He argued that shorter articles, appearing more frequently on the editorial pages with a variety of signatures, would go further in demonstrating a "large consensus of opinion."

He also issued the following caution: "By the way, would it not be wise not to mention in your accounts the checks you send me? Reporters [might be] apt to get onto it and it wouldn't help us any." Rather than keep a straight set of accounts in this regard, why not, "if consistent, [have] some individual…sign [the] check instead of the League."[29] While the league officers may have seen politics and business as synonymous, governed by the same rules, Magennis knew better. Indeed, his wisdom paralleled that of former mayor Carroll F. Sweet, who had earlier admonished the league never to reveal its executive leadership or the authorship of any of the materials it distributed throughout the city.

For the election of April 1917, Magennis wrote forty "articles" exceeding 16,000 words, for which he received regular payments of at least $20, although no record exists of the total amount he was paid. Hatten's understanding with Magennis regarding fees and services never became explicit, except for those occasions when Hatten would order up another "$10 worth of work." Payment came sporadically, and Magennis chafed at the shabby treatment, often writing the league to press for payment. "By the way," ran a familiar refrain, "if convenient to you may I take the liberty to suggest that a check at the near date would be very acceptable, as I am uncomfortably short this week?"[30]

In the spring of 1918, Hatten wrote in appreciation of Magennis's "splendid letter" to the *Evening Press,* promising to retain him for $10 and offering assurances that "we may be able eventually to do better as the needs and facilities materialize."[31] Desperate for some cash, Magennis reminded his boss, "Re the ten dollars, it will be acceptable anytime, or would a statement be required? Avoid this if you can — unless just for 'services.'"[32] Hatten strung out the $10 and $20 payments to Magennis at a time when his own salary as the league's executive secretary exceeded $4,000 a year, an amount more than twice the average skilled worker's yearly wage.

A Wall of Exclusion

Despite its efforts at image making, the league could not sustain unchallenged power for long. Eventually criticism rained down from both inside the organization itself and outside from city residents. From one member of the league's executive committee, Ralph Tietsort, furniture manufacturer and banker, came the complaint that although league membership ran to nearly 8,000 on paper, there was no serious grass-roots support or enthusiasm. Why, he wanted to know, was there no full participation beyond a cash contribution? Angered by this indifference, Tietsort demanded, "How dare they fling a fee...and say 'God Bless you' and 'Go Ahead'" without getting "out into the fight themselves!"[33]

Another executive committee member, James T. Etheridge, declared that there was an icy wall of exclusion surrounding all those who ran the league. Even though the league did good work, "the cooperation of members" should be solicited on a regular basis. "It was a mistake," Etheridge wrote, to have a "coterie of individuals forming an executive committee headed by an executive secretary" lock out not only the league's rank and file, but also its important sponsors, from the decision-making process. "If in some way the League could have more active support in its purpose by a large number of people, its influence would be increased and made more effective."

Occasionally, angry letters arrived at league offices after a mass mailing for funds had gone out. One T. J. Weber fired back to the league, "Please be advised that I personally have never been in sympathy with the organization. As a citizen and tax payer of Grand Rapids, I have failed to notice any accomplishments...of sufficient merit warranting financial support." Weber further accused the league of numerous "mud slinging" campaigns and "corrupt methods."[34] Unshaken, league president James Schouten replied that an "organized effort" was the only way to maintain good government in the city, and by the way, could Weber give some money to the league whose financial problems are "at the present time…very serious."[35]

Not all the anger came in formal correspondence. One of the more interesting retorts came from an anonymous resident who gave the league a piece of his mind in a lengthy note written in pencil on the back side of a campaign flyer that had been hung from a doorknob. "Yes, you have done fine with our money. $25,000 for a farm that was worth $8,000 [a reference to the controversial purchase of additional land for John Ball Park] – you have paid $75.00 per day…in favor of bonding the city for parks and stadium when taxes are so high that some people must lose their homes. …You would get a larger vote if you would cut out the Citizens League," the note continued. "I hear plenty of voters say they will not vote for men that your league picks out, if I [had] more paper I could give you 40 more reasons." The unhappy writer then stuffed the flyer into an envelope and mailed it back to the league.[36] An even more emphatic response came from the printer A. S. White, who published catalogs for the furniture industry. In large handwriting scrawled across the bottom of a fund-raising letter White wrote simply, "I am out of sympathy with the management of the League," and sent it back.[37]

Even in the face of rising criticism, league leadership did nothing except point up the obvious social divisions in the city. Noting that hilltop residents dominated the Board of Education, which had only a single representative from the West Side, the executive committee commented that the West Side was "almost entirely a community of wage earners," a situation that has given "rise to sectional feeling which ought, if possible to be alleviated."[38] Ironically, it was precisely this sectional feeling that had animated reformers to promote the new charter in the first place and bring about the changes that would effectively disenfranchise the West Side.

The league remained content to have its way in a divided city safely partitioned by the Grand River, dominated by commissioners who were elected at large, and nominated and funded by the league's organized support. A persistently autocratic manner characterized the league's operation, and its outlook counted bottom-line results at the ballot box as the most important measure of success. Supported by the conservative values of many Grand Rapids voters, the business community preferred to disdain grass-roots politics as it pushed its conservative agenda to control city government.

In the face of growing resentment of its tactics and constant fund raising, the league was unable to cultivate continuing support or contributions from large numbers of voters. Its seven-year struggle to maintain control ended in 1923 when modest initiatives, championed by former mayor Ellis and others since shortly after the adoption of the new charter in 1916, finally succeeded at the polls. In a narrow victory, voters approved changing the city commission from seven at-large representatives to one at-large representative and six ward-based representatives, two from each ward. The same election also brought approval for charter amendments providing for the at-large election of the mayor, city attorney, and city clerk. While not a devastating blow to the league's interests, the election results brought a greater degree of direct democracy and public accountability to the operation of the city government.[39]

In analyzing the election results, the Citizens League's city government committee complained about the lack of effective organization in turning out the vote. Unwilling even to consider the fact that the loss might have stemmed from disagreement with the league's position, or popular discontent, it never occurred to the leadership that even the established ruse of reporting light turnout in the noon papers would not bring support for an agenda that had alienated increasing numbers of residents.

Searching for other explanations, the league looked inward and found that "two years ago the League office discovered leaks in its governing body. No sooner was action taken by the executive committee, then it was discovered that our political opponents were not only in full possession of all the facts with regard to our meetings, but were prepared to damage our program and institute opposition measures." Typical of that perspective, league leaders refused to acknowledge that their inability to sustain fund-raising and membership programs might have accounted for the vote to change the charter, not their opponents' chicanery. Working to reorganize, the executive committee suggested reducing its ranks to ensure greater confidentiality. League executives preferred not to believe that Grand Rapids residents might have come to prefer a political democracy to the corporate-like system installed by the charter of 1916.

As they sought to explain the losses incurred, league leaders made peace with their opponents. From the city government committee came the written opinion that the Citizens League "should cooperate with our city officials and exert every influence towards absolute harmony and efficiency in municipal affairs."[40]

Justifying their actions to the end, league officials handed out a lengthy mimeographed report spelling out differences between the "Political Machine" and "Organized Citizenship." Putting the best possible spin on the recent changes made to the charter, the report's author emphasized the fact that the changes were modest and that Grand Rapids citizens had consistently defeated evil "machine" politicians, thanks to the work of the Citizens League.[41]

The report chose to highlight the league's success despite the overwhelming advantages of the "machine's" tight organization at the precinct and ward levels; the use of professional politicians to influence voters; the appeal to the family vote through ward politics; the use of patronage for various political duties associated with the election; and the hiring of paid messengers and runners to turn out the vote. Even though this description might be said to fit the league as well as its opponents, the report boasted that "an aroused people, with experienced management" had instituted and maintained a commission-manager government, and the charter amendments of 1923 were minor adjustments, not drastic changes. Subsequent developments would prove otherwise.

The 1916 charter commission and the seven-year-period after the charter's adoption marked the high point for the conservative reformers who sought to change Grand Rapids in the wake of the 1911 furniture strike. Their pioneer work in the use of mass marketing to promote a political agenda stands as an important legacy. In an age before modern political action committees and national party fundraisers, the Grand Rapids Citizens League showed the way.

After losing the 1923 election, the league folded, unable to sustain the fund raising and membership campaigns of its initial years, but bowing out with the knowledge that even though limited changes had been imposed, the East Side — with its hilltop leadership, two wards, and four commissioners — would continue to have a major voice in city politics. As the industrial and business leaders abandoned the league, they remained confident in their ability to exercise power. Subsequent decades have upheld that notion. For nearly a century, Grand Rapids politics has featured a balance of power and lack of corruption that would make the original reformers proud. At the same time, powerful individuals have served as mayor, putting the stamp of their personality on the city, and no one who seeks to be mayor dares ignore the potent West Side vote.

Endnotes

1. Constitution and Bylaws, Grand Rapids Citizens League Papers, collection 51, box 1: folder 1, Grand Rapids Public Library (hereafter cited as GRPL with collection, box and folder numbers, eg. 51-1-1).
2. Carroll F. Sweet to C. Roy Hatten, December 13, 1916, GRPL, 51-5-69.
3. Jeffrey Kleiman, "The Rule From Above: Businessmen, Bankers and the Drive to Organize in Grand Rapids, Michigan 1890-1906," *Michigan Historical Review* 12 (Fall 1986): pp. 45-68.
4. Contributors List, 1916, GRPL, 51-4-46. The significance of soliciting women's votes is spelled out in greater detail in Aileen Kraditor, *The Ideas of the Women's Suffrage Movement* (N. Y.: Norton, 1981).
5. Form letter from Russell Griffen, April 30, 1921, GRPL, 51-1-9.
6. Hatten Memo, [n.d]., GRPL, 51-1-15.
7. Citizen's League Membership Drive, June 3, 4, 5, 1917, and 1917 Members Not Renewed [n. d.], GRPL, 51-4-45.
8. "Contract," February 10, 1919, GRPL, 51-6-83; Executive Board Report "Finances," September 16, 1923; September 24, 1923, GRPL, 51-1-8.
9. Joel Barlow to Charles W. Garfield, March 18, 1919, GRPL, 51-2-21.
10. Schouten to Russell Griffen, October 19, 1923, GRPL, 51-3-30.
11. H. C. Cornelius to Hatten, May 17, 1918, GRPL, 51-2-21.
12. Untitled donor list, [1917], GRPL, 51-4-46.
13. Subscription and Guarantee List, May 7, 1919, GRPL, 51-2-23, 25; 51-3-29.
14. Subscription Pledge List, March 12, 1923, GRPL, 51-16-221; Subscription List [1923], GRPL, 51-1-11; Subscriptions to Date, November 3, 1924, GRPL, 51-2-17; A. P. Lovett to Hatten, March 25, 1918, GRPL, 51-7-88.
15. Collector of the IRS to John W. Blodgett, November 27, 1920, and December 7, 1920, GRPL, 51-2-25.

16. Report of the Secretary to the Executive Board, Spring, 1923, GRPL, 51-1-15.

17. Hatten to Woodruff, April 19, 1917, GRCL Papers, b. 6, f. 218; Z. Z. Lydens, *The Story of Grand Rapids,* 1966, pp. 71,75.

18. Hatten to Lovett, April 12, 1917, GRPL, 51-16-218.

19. Suggestions to Automobile Workers, 1919-1920, GRPL, 51-3-115. See also Memo, April 1, 1920, GRPL, 51-8-107.

20. Frank L. Dykema, "A Record of the Development of the Grand Rapids Americanization Society's Plan of Citizenship Training Through the Ballot," *Michigan Historical Magazine* 6 (Winter 1922): 160-74.

21. Hatten to Lovett, April 12, 1917, GRPL, 51-16-218.

22. Russell Griffen Memo, [1920], GRPL, 51-8-116; for the International Order of Odd Fellows list see GRPL, 51-8-105 to 107.

23. Hatten to Woodruff, April 19, 1917, GRPL, 51-2-218.

24. Executive Committee Minutes, April 1, 1921, GRPL, 51-1-9.

25. Hatten Memo, [1923], GRPL, 51-1-15.

26. Hatten to Woodruff, March 18, 1918, GRPL, 51-5-69; April 19, 1917, 51-2-218.

27. Unsigned memo, May 3, 1918, GRPL, 51, 1-9.

28. Disbursements During Election, March 12, 1917-April 6, 1917, GRPL, 51-9-118; Minutes of Joint Committee, August 9, 1918, GRPL, 51-5-5; general receipts, March 14, 1918, GRPL, 51-16-219; "Disbursements for Primary Campaign," April 6, 1919, GRPL, 51-9-118; George Walker to Hatten, n. d., GRPL, 51-8-115; Memo, January 4, 1922, GRPL, 51-1-10.

29. Magennis to Hatten, March 19, 1917, GRPL, 51-16-218.

30. Ibid. March 21, 1917, March 22, 1917, March 26, 1917, GRPL, 51-16-218.

31. Hatten to Magennis, June 18, 1918,GRPL, 51-3-36.

32. Magennis to Hatten, June 21, 1918, GRPL, 51-3-36.

33. Secretary's Report, September 23, 1920, GRPL, 51-2-20.

34. Weber to Garfield, November 18, 192 1, GRPL, 51-1-14.

35. Schouten to Garfield, December 14, 1921, GRPL, 51-1-14.

36. A Vital Message, [April 1, 1922], GRPL, 51-5-72.

37. White to League, October 31, 1924, GRPL, 51-2-17.

38. Minutes of the Executive Board, March 18, 1919, GRPL, 51-1-6.

39. Jeffrey Kleiman, "Worker Response to Progressive Municipal Reform 1917-1927," Great Lakes History Conference, Grand Rapids, MI (April 1987).

40. Report of the Executive Committee, October 30, 1923, GRPL, 51-1-11.

41. Untitled report, October 8, 1924, GRPL, 51-2-17.

Bibliography

PRIMARY SOURCES

Grand Rapids Citizens League Papers, Grand Rapids Public Library.

Minutes of the Grand Rapids Board of Trade Board of Directors Meetings, Bound copies in the Grand Rapids Public Library.

PUBLISHED SOURCES

Books

Bartow, Josef, *Peasants and Strangers: Italians, Rumanians and Slovaks in an American City* (Cambridge, Harvard University Press, 1975).

Bodnar, John, *The Transplanted* (Bloomington, Indiana University Press, 1985).

Boorstin, Daniel, *The Genius of American Politics* (Chicago, University of Chicago Press, 1953).

Bratt, James D., *Dutch Calvinism in Modern America: A History of a Conservative Subculture* (Grand Rapids, William B. Eerdmans Publishing Company, 1984).

Brecher, Jeremy, *Strike* (Boston, South End Press, 1977).

Brody, David, *Steelworkers in America: The Nonunion Era* (New York, Harper Torchbooks, 1960).

Bucket Shop Department Store, (Good Government League of Grand Rapids, n.d.). Copy in the Grand Rapids History and Special Collections Center of the Grand Rapids Public Library.

Buenker, John D., *Urban Liberation and Progressive Reform* (New York, Scribners, 1973).

Cannon, James, *Clearing Houses: Their History, Methods and Administration* (New York, D. Appleton and Co., 1900)

Chandler, Alfred D., *The Visible Hand* (Cambridge, Harvard University Press, 1977).

Christie, Robert, *Empire in Wood* (Ithaca, Cornell University Press, 1956).

Cowing, Cedric, *Populists, Plungers and Progressives: A Social History of Stock and Commodity Speculation* (Princeton, Princeton University Press, 1969).

Dau's Blue Book and Social Reporter for Grand Rapids (Chicago, Dau's Blue Book Inc., 1906).

Dorau, Herbert B., and Albert G. Hinman, *Urban Land Economics* (New York, Macmillan, 1928).

Douglas, Paul, *Real Wages in the United States 1890-1926* (Boston, Houghton Mifflin Company, 1930).

Edel, Matthew, Elliot D. Sclar and Daniel Luria, *Shaky Palaces* (New York, Columbia University Press, 1984).

Ewen, Linda, *Corporate Power and Urban Crisis in Detroit* (Princeton, N.J., Princeton University Press, 1978).

Fine, Nathan, *Labor and Farmer Parties in the United States* (New York, Rand School of Social Science 1928).

Flaherty, Viva, *History of the Grand Rapids Furniture Strike* (n.p., 1911), p. 21. Copy in the Grand Rapids History and Special Collections Center of the Grand Rapids Public Library.

George Ellis as Juggler, (Grand Rapids by the Good Government League, 1914-1916).

Grand Rapids City Directory, (Polk Publishing Company, Detroit, 1912).

Grebler, Leo, et al., *Capital Formation in Residential Real Estate* (Princeton, Princeton University Press, 1956).

Greene, Victor, *For God and Country: The Rise of Polish and Lithuanian Ethnic Consciousness in America 1860-1910* (Madison, State Historical Society of Wisconsin, 1975).

Gusfield, Joseph R., *Symbolic Crusade: Status Politics and the American Temperance Movement* (Urbana, University of Illinois Press, 1966).

Hartz, Louis, *The Liberal Tradition in America* (New York, Harcourt, Brace & World, 1955).

Hays, Samuel P., *The Response to Industrialism* (Chicago, University of Chicago Press, 1957).

Higham, John, *Strangers in the Land* (New York, Atheneum, 1972).

Holli, Melvin, *Reform in Detroit* (New York, Oxford University Press, 1967).

Horowitz, Morris A., *The Structure and Government of the Carpenters' Union* (New York, John Wiley and Sons, 1962).

James, John A., *Money and Capital Markets in Postbellum America* (Princeton, Princeton University Press, 1978)

Kirkland, Edward C., *Dream and Thought in the Business Community* (Ithaca, Cornell University Press, 1956).

Kolko, Gabriel, *The Triumph of Conservatism* (New York, Quadrangle Books, 1962).

Korman, Gerd, *Industrialization, Immigrants and Americanizers: The View From Milwaukee, 1866-1921* (Madison, State Historical Society of Wisconsin, 1967).

Kraditor, Aileen, *The Ideas of the Women's Suffrage Movement* (New York, Norton, 1981).

Kraditor, Aileen, *The Radical Persuasion: 1890-1917* (Baton Rouge, Louisiana State University Press, 1981).

Kromminga, John, *The Christian Reformed Church: A Study in Orthodoxy* (Grand Rapids, Baker Book House, 1949).

Kroos, Herman E., and Martin R. Blyn, *The History of Financial Intermediaries* (New York, Random House, 1971).

Letwin, William, *Law and Economic Policy in America: The Evolution of the Sherman Anti-Trust Act* (New York, Random House, 1965).

Lydens, Z. Z., *The Story of Grand Rapids* (Grand Rapids, Kregel Publishing Co., 1966).

May, Henry L., *Protestant Churches and Industrial America* (New York, Harper & Brothers, 1949).

McGee, John, *The Catholic Church in the Grand River Valley* (Grand Rapids, St. Andrews Cathedral, 1950).

Milispaugh, Arthur C., *Party Organization and Machinery in Michigan Since 1890* (Baltimore, Johns Hopkins University Press, 1917).

Mizruchi, Mark S., *The American Corporate Network 1904-1974* (Beverly Hills, Sage Publications, 1982).

Moody's Manual of Industrial and Miscellaneous Securities, (New York, John Moody & Company, 1908).

Moody's Manual of Municipal Bonds, (New York, John Moody & Company, 1922).

National Cyclopedia of Biography.

National Housing Association, *Housing Problems in America* (Cambridge, Harvard University Press, 1913).

Pred, Allan R. *The Spatial Dynamics of U.S. Urban-Industrial Growth, 1800-1914* (Cambridge, MIT Press, 1966).

Ransom, Frank E., *The City Built on Wood: A History of the Furniture Industry in Grand Rapids, Michigan 1850-1950* (Ann Arbor, Edwards Brothers, Michigan, 1955).

Ratner, Sidney, Richard Sylla and James Soltow, *The Evolution of the American Economy* (New York, Basic Books, 1979).

Rees, Albert, *Real Wages in Manufacturing 1890-1914* (Princeton, Princeton University Press, 1961).

Repudiated by Republicans: Ellis Has Never Received the Full Vote of the Party (Grand Rapids, Good Government League of Grand Rapids, 1914-1916).

Rice, Bradley R., *Progressive Cities: The Commission Government Movement in America 1901-1920* (Austin, University of Texas Press, 1977).

Rosenblum, Gerald, *Immigrant Workers: Their Impact on American Labor Radicalism* (New York, Basic Books, 1973).

Sarasohn, Stephen B. and Vera H., *Political Parties in Michigan* (Detroit, Wayne State University Press, 1957).

Schiesl, Martin J., *The Politics of Efficiency: Municipal Administration and Reform in America 1880-1920* (Berkeley, 1972).

Sennett, Richard, *Families Against the City: Middle-Class Homes of Industrial Chicago: 1872-1890* (Cambridge, Harvard University Press, 1970).

Sidelights on George Ellis. (Grand Rapids, Good Government League of Grand Rapids, 1914-1916).

Some Racy Reading, (Grand Rapids, Good Government League of Grand Rapids, 1914).

Sparks, Frank M., *The Business of Government Municipal Reform,* (Chicago, 1916).

Stein, Herbert, *The Fiscal Revolution in America* (Chicago, University of Chicago Press, 1969).

Sylla, Richard, *The American Capital Market 1846-1914* (North Stratford, New Hampshire, Ayer Publishing Co., 1979).

Thernstrom, Stephen, *Poverty and Progress* (Cambridge, Harvard University Press, 1964).

Thomas' Register of American Manufacturers (New York, Thomas Publishing Co., 1914).

Trescott, Paul B., *Financing American Enterprise* (New York, Harper and Row, 1963).

Ward, David, *Cities and Immigrants: A Geography of Change in the Nineteenth Century* (New York, Oxford University Press, 1971).

White, Ronald C., and C. Howard Hopkins, *The Social Gospel: Religion and Reform in Changing America* (Philadelphia, Temple University Press, 1976).

Wiebe, Robert, *The Search for Order* (New York, Hill and Wang, 1967).

Wishart, Alfred W. "Sermon Preached January 13, 1907" (n.p., n.d.). Copy in the Grand Rapids History and Special Collections Center of the Grand Rapids Public Library.

Wishart, Alfred W. *The Social Mission of the Church* (American Baptist Social Service Commission of the Northern Baptist Convention, 1909).

Wishart, Alfred W., "Industrial Democracy: An Address Delivered before the National Furniture Manufacturers Association in Grand Rapids, December 1, 1915," (n.p., n.d.). Copy in the Grand Rapids History and Special Collections Center of the Grand Rapids Public Library.

Zunz, Oliver, *The Changing Face of Inequality* (Chicago, University of Chicago Press, 1982).

Zwaanstra, Henry, *Reformed Thought and Experience in a New World* (Amsterdam, J. H. Kok, 1973).

Articles

Abell, Aaron I., "American Catholic Response to Industrial Conflict: The Arbital Process 1885-1900," *The Catholic Historical Review* XLVI, no. 4 (January, 1956)

Abramson, Harold, "Ethnic Diversity Within Catholicism," *Journal of Social History* 4 (1971).

Allen, Michael, "The Structure of Interorganizational Elite Cooperation: Interlocking Directorates," *American Sociological Review* 39 (1974).

Bradshaw, James, "Grand Rapids Furniture Beginnings," *Michigan History* 52 (Winter, 1968).

Bradshaw, James, "Grand Rapids, 1870-1880: The Furniture City," *Michigan History* 55 (Winter, 1971).

Dooley, Peter C., "The Interlocking Directorate," *American Economic Review* 59 (1969).

Dubovsky, Melvin, *We Shall Be All: A History of the Industrial Workers of the World* (Champagne-Urbana: University of Illinois Press, 1988).

Dykema, Frank L., "A Record of the Development of the Grand Rapids Americanization Society's Plan of Citizenship Training Through the Ballot," *Michigan Historical Magazine* 6 (Winter 1922).

Elenbaas, Jack D., "The Boss of the Better Class: Henry Leland and the Detroit Citizens League, 1912-1924," *Michigan History* 58 (Spring, 1974).

Fisher, Ernest M., and Raymond F. Smith, "Land Subdividing and the Rate of Utilization," *Michigan Business Studies* 4 (1932).

Fragnoli, Raymond R., "Progressive Coalition and Municipal Reform: Charter Revision in Detroit 1912-1918," *Detroit in Perspective: A Journal of Regional History* 4 (Spring, 1980).

Frisch, Michael, "Oyez, Oyez, Oyez: The Recurring Case of *Plunkett v. Steffens,*" *Journal of Urban History* 7 (February, 1981).

Gould, Stephen Jay, *The Mismeasure of Man* (New York, W. W. Norton & Company, 1982).

Gutman, Herbert, "Class, Status and Community Power in Nineteenth Century Industrial Cities: Paterson, New Jersey: A Case Study" in *Work, Culture and Society in Industrializing America* (New York, Random House, 1976).

Hays, Samuel P., "The Changing Political Structure of the City in Industrial America," *Journal of Urban History* 1 (November, 1974).

Hutchinson, William R., "Cultural Strain and Protestant Liberalism," *American Historical Review* 76 (April, 1971).

John S. MacDonald, "Urbanization, Ethnic Groups and Social Segmentation," *Social Research* 29 (Winter, 1962),

Kirk, Carolyn, and Gordon Kirk, "Impact of the City on Home Ownership," *Journal of Urban History* 7 (August 1981).

Kleiman, Jeffrey, "The Rule from Above: Businessmen, Bankers and the Drive to Organize in Grand Rapids, Michigan 1890-1906," *Michigan Historical Review* 12 (Fall 1986).

Luker, Ralph E., "The Social Gospel and the Failure of Radical Reform, 1877-1898," *Church History* 46 (March, 1977).

Lurie, Jonathan, "Private Association, Internal Regulation and Progressivism: The Chicago Board of Trade, 1880-1923, as a Case Study," *American Journal of Legal History* 16 (1977).

Mapes, Lynn G., "Flamboyant Mayor George Ellis," *Grand Rapids Magazine* (January, 1976).

Marusen, Ann R., "Class and Urban Social Expenditure: A Marxist Theory of Metropolitan Government" in William K. Tabb and Larry Sawers, eds., *Marxism and the Metropolis: New Perspectives in Urban Political Economy* (New York, Oxford University Press, 1978).

Pinkowski, Edward, "The Great Influx of Polish Immigrants and the Industries They Entered" in Frank Mocha, ed., *Poles in America: Bicentennial Essays* (Stevens Point, Worzalla Publishing, 1978).

Scott, Thomas A., "The Diffusion of Urban Governmental Forms as a Case Study of Social Learning," *Journal of Politics* 30 (1968).

Skendzel, Eduard Adam, "The Polanders," *Grand River Valley Review,* Vol. IV, No. 2, Spring/Summer 1983.

Stone, Michael E., "Housing, Mortgage Lending and the Contradictions of Capitalism," in William K. Tabb and Larry Sawers, eds., *Marxism and the Metropolis: New Perspectives in Urban Political Economy* (New York, Oxford University Press, 1978).

Swierenga, Robert F., "The Dutch in West Michigan: The Impact of a Contractual Community," *Grand River Valley History,* Vol. 18, 2001.

Szaz, Ferenc, "Protestantism and the Search for Stability: Liberal and Conservative Quests for a Christian America, 1875-1925" in Jerry Israel, ed., *Building the Organizational Society* (New York, Free Press, 1970).

Travis, Anthony R., "Mayor George Ellis: Grand Rapids Political Boss and Progressive Reformer," *Michigan History* 58 (Spring, 1974).

Unpublished Sources

Skendzel, Eduard Adam, "Polonian Musings," (photocopied typescript in the Grand Rapids History and Special Collections Center, Grand Rapids Public Library).

Vanderstel, David G., "The Dutch of Grand Rapids, Michigan 1848-1900: Immigrant Neighborhoods and Community Development in a Nineteenth-Century City," (unpublished Ph.D. dissertation, Kent State University, 1983).

Kleiman, Jeffrey, "Worker Response to Progressive Municipal Reform 1917-1927," paper presented at the Great Lakes History Conference, Grand Rapids, MI (April 1987).

Kurzhals, Richard D., "Initial Advantage and Technological Change in Industrial Location: The Furniture Industry in Grand Rapids, Michigan" (unpublished Ph.D. dissertation, Michigan State University, 1973).

Schulte, Frank J., "Municipal Personnel Administration: City of Grand Rapids," 1970. (bound copy in the Grand Rapids History and Special Collections Center, Grand Rapids Public Library).

Faires, Nora, "Ethnicity in Evolution: The German Community in Pittsburgh and Allegheny City, Pennsylvania 1845-1885" (unpublished Ph.D. dissertation, University of Pittsburgh, 1981).

Newspapers, Magazines and Trade Journals
Civic News (Grand Rapids, Michigan)
Creston News
Detroit Free Press
Furniture Designer
Furniture Manufacturer and Artisan
Grand Rapids Evening Press
Grand Rapids Herald
Grand Rapids News
Grand Rapids Progress
Michigan Tradesman
Milwaukee Journal
Outlook
Solidarity
The Observer (Grand Rapids, Michigan)

Government Documents
City Charter of the City of Grand Rapids, 1905.

Department of Commerce, Bureau of Census, *Mortgages on Homes: Report on the Results of the Inquiry as to the Mortgage Debt on Homes Other than Farm Homes at the Fourteenth Census* (Washington, D.C., U.S. Government Printing Office, 1923).

Federal Trade Commission, *Report on the House-Furnishings Industry,* Vol. 1, (Washington, D.C., U.S. Government Printing Office, 1923).

Michigan Department of Labor, *Annual Reports,* 1900, 1902, 1904, 1908, 1911.

Michigan State Census Reports, 1890, 1894, 1900, 1904.

Minutes of the Grand Rapids Charter Commission, 1915. Copy in the Grand Rapids History and Special Collections Center, Grand Rapids Public Library.

Report of the Commissioner of the Banking Department of the State of Michigan (Lansing, 1912).

Report of the Immigration Commission (Washington, D.C., U.S. Government Printing Office, 1911), Vol. 15.

U.S. Bureau of the Census, *Special Bulletin,* no. 18; Department of Commerce and Labor, *Census of Manufacturers.*

U.S. Bureau of the Census, Twelfth Federal Census, *Manufacturers.*

Websites
McCusker, John J., "Comparing the Purchasing Power of Money in the United States (or Colonies) from 1665 to Any Other Year Including the Present," *Economic History Services,* 2004 <http://www.eh.net/hmit/ppowerusd/>.

Index